D0369124

ALL IN MY HEAD

ALL IN MY HEAD

A memoir of life, love and patient power

JESSICA MORRIS

FLEET
2022

FLEET

First published in Great Britain in 2022 by Fleet

1 3 5 7 9 10 8 6 4 2

A CIP catalogue record for this book is available from the British Library.

Hardback ISBN 978-0-349-72683-0
Trade paperback format ISBN 978-0-349-72682-3

Typeset in Garamond by M Rules
Printed and bound in Great Britain by
Clays Ltd, Elcograf S.p.A.

Papers used by Fleet are from well-managed forests and other responsible sources.

Fleet
An imprint of
Little, Brown Book Group
Carmelite House
50 Victoria Embankment
London EC4Y 0DZ

An Hachette UK Company
www.hachette.co.uk

www.littlebrown.co.uk

Contents

For Ed, Felix, Tess and Emma

1

A Waldorf Wobble

I didn't choose jazz, jazz chose me.

That's the first line of the wonderful British jazz musician George Melly's autobiography, *Rum, Bum and Concertina*. At least, it is according to me.

There is an after-dinner game that some people know as 'the book game'; fancier players refer to it as 'Ex Libris'. Players are given a book's title and author, and its year of publication. Everyone drafts their own imaginary first line. These are put into a hat, along with the genuine first line. Someone reads them all out, and the players vote for which they think is the real one.

The actual first line of George Melly's autobiography doesn't do justice to his incredible life, wit and abundant creative talent. I seem to recall it is something dull about prep school. I like to think mine – 'I didn't choose jazz, jazz chose me' – was a posthumous gift for him. And, as it turns out, for me.

Because: I didn't choose cancer. Cancer chose me.

This business of bodies is an odd one. Over half a century of life, and I'm still struggling. I see my physical and psychological selves as overlapping circles, a Venn diagram in perpetual motion, competing for my attention. For most of my life, the psychological me has grabbed my consciousness like a tabloid headline; the physical me has been sidelined to the classified ads in a local magazine gathering dust on the coffee table. Assumed to be healthy, mostly ignored. I've seen my body as a workhorse, strong and functional, not attractive aesthetically, but more than does the job. It tends not to allow illness, bugs, viruses, or anything horrible. What I didn't expect was that it could turn on itself, from the inside.

My body's suicide mission revealed itself on 23 January 2016, at around 4 pm – at the top of a hill.

In the Catskills in upstate New York, nestled in a valley, is a picture-perfect inn with a large veranda. Inside the Beaverkill Valley Inn are cosy rooms with log fires. It oozes comfort and warmth. We go every year to this oasis, a tradition started by friends who got married there. They invited us to a group weekend in 2007, just a year after we moved to New York from London. It was such a hit that we've been coming together, around ten families in all, every year since.

This particular year, there wasn't the usual abundance of snow, and the cross-country skiing had to be put on hold. We were itching to get outside, so I joined forces with three girlfriends and we set off for a hike up the hill. I was a little uncomfortable because my snow jacket was too large, as were my gloves. By contrast, my snow boots were too tight. I felt weighed down before we had even started. Nonetheless we set off, leaving behind the rest of the pack as they sat around the fire playing Bananagrams. We chatted, while our bodies adapted to the cold and our eyes grew accustomed to the brightness of a patchy landscape of miserly snow framed by a dull white sky.

I felt good, safe and happy in the company of these friends whom I never see enough. We upped our pace gently. Alex, who is proportioned like a gazelle, strode ahead. We were reaching a crossroads, and it was time to decide whether to go on or turn back. Alex wanted to go on, Gretchen and Janet were undecided. I was feeling a guilty urge to retreat to the inn, my book and the enticing fireplace. Why did I feel so burdened and tired? I answered myself silently, knowing my answer to the question was the usual self-denigrating one: it must be because I was overweight.

Wait. Something else. Something inexplicably odd. Within seconds, odder still. I could feel myself growing even more tired and somehow – intangibly – different from how I would normally feel on a walk like this. That feeling of being extra tired must have been here for a reason, but it was not a reason I could understand. I was confused about whether I wanted to go on, or whether this strange feeling meant I should turn back. I opened my mouth to say something, while knowing that I wasn't sure what I wanted to say. There was something impeding my fluency of thought and speech.

I have a tendency to talk too much. Right now, I needed to at least say whether I wanted to walk on or turn around. But I was stuck, like a mouse on a glue board.

Speaking out loud can open the gates to my mind, much as others find meditating silently takes them to new levels of self-awareness and appreciation. I felt as if I were struggling to call out during a nightmare. It was a strange combination – feeling out of control, yet sensing a baton being slowly and inexorably passed to a stranger. The sensation of trying to make myself heard, and the terror of not being able to.

I opened my mouth. There was a disconnect between my desire to say something – anything – and my ability to do so. 'Agh . . . ' I managed, weakly.

I could see Janet's face, smiling, but concerned and confused: 'Just take your time, Jess, and try again.' I tried to breathe calmly, control slipping away. I looked at Alex and Gretchen's faces. They had the same look of confusion. 'Agh . . . ' said the mouse.

And then I saw my eyelids close.

When I regained consciousness, Eric and Josh and other friends were gathered around. Their faces were calm, serious, warm, trying to mask fear. Everything was white. White snow, white sky. An image of the bright lights used in torture scenes flickered across my mind. I felt a sense of relief, which I knew was unwarranted, but I didn't know why. Eric steered me into a small vehicle. Everyone was focused on me. I knew something had happened to me. Then I saw my husband Ed, and I grabbed his hand and felt the fear come down a notch.

Somewhere we transferred to an ambulance. I was lying down, a smiling paramedic sitting by me. I remember her dark navy jacket, and her glossy black hair pulled into a ponytail. She had a cheery manner, and rested her hand on my shoulder as she chatted away – I think she was talking about her boyfriend – just enough to stop me thinking about what had happened, but not enough to engage me fully. I was slowly becoming more conscious, more enquiring, more sanely scared. No white lights, just creeping, sober fear. I knew I was still on Planet Earth, but also that a tectonic plate had shifted.

I was told I'd had a seizure while hiking. I couldn't begin to process this information. My face was rigid, presenting an artificial default setting of a slight smile. I was given a CT scan. I had to lie with my head in a case to immobilise it, then I was gradually moved, electronically, into a donut. It felt suspiciously like a coffin, I thought fleetingly, remembering a terrifying TV film of a young woman who'd been buried alive somewhere in America. I made a conscious effort to look away from the memories of bad films and delve into a familiar childhood scene. I am in Greenwich Park, in London, where I spent much of my childhood. I am on my bike, riding up the central path, veering left at the top, then right to go deep down and then immediately up, making sure I go downhill fast enough to have the necessary power to come back without having to pedal.

When the CT scan was finished I was told, somewhat matter-of-factly, that there was 'something' there and that I would need an MRI, the more powerful imaging using magnetic fields, the next day. I might also need surgery.

What?

When I was eight, I sliced the top of the fourth finger on my right hand just about off. One moment I was unfolding a metal chair, the next I was staring at a bit of my anatomy that was dangling from the rest of my body by three-sixteenths of an inch of tissue.

On the way to the hospital Mum cupped my hand under a flannel. I could sense she was trying to appear to me to be calm and in control, when inwardly she was a tight knot of anxiety. The junior doctor who treated me had a nervous smile which widened into a surprised grin when he managed to stitch my finger back together. I remember looking at the hair the junior doctor had draped over his bald patch, and his look of puzzlement, and thinking of Tintin's friend Cuthbert Calculus.

Many years later, Mum told me that after my finger-severing escapade I started to suck my thumb again, a habit I had given up along with nappies. My finger healed, eventually. It was perfectly functional, though not perfect. There's never a perfect heal.

A month before the seizure, in December 2015, I'd taken my then thirteen-year-old daughter Emma to tea at the Waldorf Hotel in London. We were back for Christmas, and Emma had asked to go for tea somewhere 'fancy'. Perhaps I have read too many Eloise books, but I wanted to indulge her. And myself. Memories of client-chargeable breakfasts at glamorous London hotels were itching to be resurrected. Ed and our other two children, Tess and Felix, were arriving a few days later, so I booked the tea.

I was tired. I'd been working hard and feeling increasingly stressed. For three years, I'd headed up the New York office of a UK-based corporate PR firm. I'd worked my arse off to reach what felt like crazy revenue targets, and was proud that we'd secured the magic numbers and, more importantly, that the work was interesting and meaningful. But towards the end of the year, the business had merged with a much larger entity. The New York office was not a priority. It had been a bruising experience. I was slow to come to terms with what had happened and had to forge a role in a big company that didn't really seem to know what to do with me, or even to want me. I was anxious, concerned, confused, exhausted . . . yet starting to glimpse the possibility that I could seduce both my new bosses and their clients.

After Emma and I landed at Heathrow, we went straight to my mother-in-law's house in Highbury for coffee. I ground the beans in the same old wall-mounted coffee grinder she's had all the decades I've known her, sat down, and sipped. I checked the route to the Waldorf, urged Emma to get ready, and left the kitchen to grab my coat.

I was in the hallway when I suddenly fell. I didn't know why. I hadn't tripped, and a question mark popped into my head. I decided I must be jet-lagged.

I got up, put on my coat, called Emma, and off we went. As we were walking towards the Waldorf, I felt one side of my body being slightly pulled down. It was as if gravity was stronger on one side than the other. Just as I started to feel uneasy, the sensation stopped. More jet lag, I thought.

We had a lovely tea, with China cups and little sandwiches and cakes, and I forgot all about feeling odd. It wasn't until months later that I realised that it was so not jet lag.

2

Holding Tight on the See-Saws

It took me several days to comprehend the scale of what was happening to me. I think I was in complete shock. I found myself repeatedly revisiting memories of my happy and loving childhood. Maybe my subconscious was searching for something comforting. Memories of wandering through Greenwich Park, playing with the children in my neighbourhood, and, later on, sneaking out of the house with my sister to meet up with our friends, trickled into my mind..

I was born at home, the third and last child of Liz and Bill Morris, a few months before President Kennedy was shot. My parents had both grown up by the sea. They moved to London when they married, and Greenwich, right on the Thames, represented the best of metropolitan excitement. These were the Fifties and Sixties, before 'gentrification' had even been thought of. Greenwich was full of crumbling Georgian houses, junk shops and true 'caffs'. (Nowadays, the Georgian houses are gleaming, the junk shops are antique havens and the caffs fancy restaurants.) When I think of my early years, I can't help but smile. My older brother and sister were very loving. My parents were affectionate, interesting and funny.

Greenwich was filled with extraordinary characters who helped me understand how to navigate a variety of experiences. I had friends from all walks of life, like Janice, who joined me on regular trips to steal from the shopping centre, and Flavia, who went on to work with the Royal Ballet. The array of people that I came across as a child set me up for my adult life, where no matter how much a person's character seems to differ from mine I can usually find a way to connect with them.

I grew up on a tectonic plate. If you walk along my old street you'll see the meridian line etched into the pavement. This line traces all the way up to the Royal Observatory in Greenwich Park. Since the late nineteenth century, the Prime Meridian has divided the eastern and western hemispheres of the Earth – just as the equator divides the northern and southern hemispheres. Every place on the planet is measured in terms of its angle east or west from this line. I could hopscotch over that line, from east to west, and west to east, any time I wanted. I had a choice.

When I can't sleep, I think of Greenwich. Instead of counting sheep, I walk up the steps of my childhood home, open the front door, and move from room to room. I see the William Morris wallpaper in the hallway and the pencil lines where we drew round the flowers as we chatted to friends on the phone. I see the kitchen 'bar top', half iroko and half black Formica. I walk up the stairs, sit on the sofa in the living room and enjoy the view of the park from the floor-to-ceiling windows. I get stuck on enjoying the memories provoked by images of tiny details, like the way the curtains hung in the spare room, and how comforting I found them in 1973 when Granny stayed with us during the three-day week following the coal miners' and railway workers' strike, when we had to go to bed by candlelight. I felt those curtains kept us wrapped up and safe.

It's still my home, my haven, cradling me, and I feel warmed by my memory of it. I take the mind-tour of the house slowly, relishing each detail as well as the overall vision and emotion. Sometimes, once I've ticked off every cork floor tile, made sure every picture is in place, remembered the posters of Marc Bolan and Biba on my bedroom wall and my collection of old tin boxes stuffed full of cigarette ends to hide them from my mother, I'll leave the house, cross the street and step over the meridian line to

Greenwich Park. Making a choice, which side of this wide and wild world I'm going to enter, intrigued by what I'm travelling towards as well as what I've left behind.

When our children were very young and we lived in north London, I had a recurring dream about Greenwich. The house and the park were permanent fixtures in these dreams, but the other details varied. Sometimes my parents still lived there and had invited me and Ed and the kids back to live with them, as the park was such a fantastic playground for children. Other times we were back there taking care of them, and all going to the park together. Whatever the situation, the sensations were always the same: happiness, safety and relief, friendship, a space at the centre of the world where I could give my children what I'd had – deep and constant love, and a huge, beautiful public space to explore on my own or with my family or my friends, where everyone was defined by their desire to be there, and no other labels mattered.

I lay in a daze until the next day rolled around. I was waiting for the MRI results. My mind ricocheted from calm confidence that all would be fine to an increasing certainty that the MRI would find I was riddled with cancer from top to bottom, that I was about to die, that my life was unambiguously over, any whisper of hope or choice obliterated. All my worst fears up until then were as nothing compared to how I felt in that bed at that moment.

I thought of the funny rhyme my sister made up when we were kids as a way of teasing me: 'Jessica Jane had a pain in the brain, oh dear she'll never be the same again!' I wondered if this time it was true.

I thought of my cousin and godmother Mary, who had had a benign brain tumour successfully removed some years previously.

Soon I was completely unable to think of anything other than my imminent death. I didn't think of it as a thought. I knew it to be true.

Ed and I both sighed with relief when we were told that the MRI had found one mass in my head, and that this meant I had a primary tumour. These animals, if they originate in the brain, stay in the brain and tend not to metastasise to other organs. Ed emailed our friends and family: 'It's one thing, we know what we're dealing with,' he wrote, the assumption being that this meant it would be an easier target to hit.

By now I was in a spanking new hospital in the countryside about an hour's drive north of New York City, which was the closest major hospital to the hillside where I had collapsed. I was pleased. All was clean and pristine. I was in an ICU room that had a huge window with a panoramic view of the Catskill mountains. If I had to have surgery on my brain, I wanted to have it in a sanitised environment, with a view of nature and not a scalpel in sight. Fears of hospital superbugs could surely be set aside.

Meanwhile, our friends were worried about me undergoing surgery out in Hicksville, their assumption being that the best surgeons must be in the city. One friend called an old college acquaintance who had become a prominent neurosurgeon, seeking his advice. The neurosurgeon replied: 'Are you talking about the same Jessica Morris I'm about to see in ten minutes?' An extraordinary coincidence: the person who was going to mess about in my head was connected to me by just one degree of separation. Serendipity was alive and well and on my side.

I was wheeled into the operating theatre on a gurney. I couldn't think about how I felt. I just knew that if Ed was there I could cope. I still couldn't move my facial muscles, rigid in the moment, that surreal slight smile my greeting to the world. We moved along corridors, and I lay looking up at the ceiling, feeling the movement of the gurney. I thought of my father, an architect who had designed many hospitals in his time. I wondered how he'd coped with all those curved vinyl floor corners. Why such unattractive dull pastel wall colours? And then, in the theatre, I took comfort from the inevitability of the procedure. I knew the drill. I'd had a D&C, a surgical procedure to scrape the lining of the uterus, following a miscarriage before our first child was born. I'd seen many episodes of *ER*, *Grey's Anatomy* and *Casualty*. Mask on, then going under. Absolutely nothing I could do about it. Let George Clooney do his business. I believed I would survive the operation, but perhaps that's because I didn't give it much thought. I had put on some metaphorical overalls to get me through, and a plastic smile. If I didn't come to, I wouldn't know. Ed was outside and so strong, our children so strong, our transatlantic community of family and friends so strong, it would be awful and sad, but in the grand scheme of things, what is one life, even if it is your own?

I did come to, and when I did I saw my Ed and felt an enormous sense of peace and an inner, gentle smile of happiness and relief that I was still here.

'A grape' is how the surgeon described the cluster of killer cells he'd scooped out of my head.

The operation had taken five hours. The grape had been growing evilly in the left parietal section of my brain. That's the area at the back of the head behind your left ear. The tumour was about three millimetres in diameter and situated near the surface of the brain. The surgeon was upbeat, explaining that he thought it had gone well and I seemed to be recovering quickly. I was able to walk, aided, the next day. I seemed relatively intact. I think various tests were done to see if I could see and hear and had all my other faculties. But in reality, I was mentally in a marshmallow of passive shock.

I had a twinge of doubt when the surgeon repeated the phrase 'I erred on the side of caution,' when he described what he had done. On the side of caution. What did that mean? He hadn't wanted to leave me impaired, he said, so he wasn't sure he'd got the whole thing out. Because the tumour was quite near my skull, it would be possible to go back in again at a later date if need be. Anyway, the bulk of the tumour was now out of me, and a section was being analysed by pathology, so we'd have to wait a while to know exactly what kind of tumour it was.

His tone was reassuring, but the twinge flexed inside my mind. Wasn't the point 'to get the whole thing out'? I asked him what it was like to remove. What did it look like? He described it as like removing vanilla ice-cream from a sea of mayonnaise. Ah, I thought, now I get why you people are so venerated. My father-in-law was a professor of medicine, my mother-in-law a psychiatrist. They were condescending about surgery, equating it with carpentry. As the daughter and sister of an architect and a carpenter, I saw this analogy as a positive. I wouldn't have trusted my in-laws to spot the difference between vanilla ice-cream and mayonnaise. My family by contrast could quite happily (and often did) talk about different shades of white paint for the entire evening.

The surgeon said he would refer me to New York University. He thought it likely that I would need a six-week course of combined radiotherapy and chemotherapy, followed by a further six months of chemotherapy. The word cancer wasn't uttered. So I chose not to hear it.

We stayed in the hospital for two days. I felt better by

the minute. I was deeply comfortable, lying in a state-of-the-art bed that prodded my body gently whenever part of me lay still for too long, presumably to avoid bed sores. And being a woman *d'un certain âge*, I rather liked having a catheter – it saved me from having to go to the loo all the time. Ed was in a ridiculously comfortable chair beside me, a sort of twenty-first-century version of a Parker Knoll throne, and was able to sleep there right next to me at night. Friends visited with reassuring faces. Lovely nurses took care of us both, the telly murmured in the background, and we dozed.

Ed's bosses told him to take all the time he needed. My employers, with whom I'd spent less than a month, were adult, empathetic, generous and caring. My mother, living in the UK, asked Ed how long he could take care of me during what might be a very disrupted period. He answered: 'I'm here for the duration.'

When I was fourteen, a year older than my daughter Emma was when I had my first seizure, I knocked my front teeth out while attempting a backflip in Greenwich swimming pool. Apart from the incident with the little finger, this was the biggest health challenge I'd had until that point. Fourteen can be a difficult age, and as I reflect on how well Emma seemed to cope with her mother facing a major health crisis at that age, I feel great pride in her and a little bit in me.

My friend Imogen, who lived next door to us in Greenwich, had been with me when the teeth incident happened. I'd just learned how to stand on the edge of the pool with my back to it, jump up and backwards, and turn full circle into the water. I enjoyed the sensation of envisioning the move and then being able to realise it, my mind and body in perfect harmony. The first time I did it, one of the other girls with us was too nervous to try, and I remember one of the boys saying, 'Look at Jess, she'll try anything.' I hadn't thought of myself like that, but I liked hearing it.

The next week, Imogen and I were there on our own. I stood on the edge of the pool, my back to the water, and felt unexpectedly confused. I wasn't feeling the mind–body harmony. Should I pinch my nose, or would I need both hands free? What had I done last time? I leapt and dived, not going far out enough and as a result crash-landing as I came full circle to the side of the pool. Somewhere on the bottom my two front teeth lay looking up at me accusingly.

Until then, I had felt my body worked well. I remember being in the school gym and knowing during netball sessions that I could put the ball into the net. I was a strong and fast swimmer, having mastered the art of working with and against the water. I wasn't particularly talented, but I felt I occupied a body that at least was functional.

The broken teeth smashed that self-image. The

happiness and ease of my youth took its biggest punch the moment my front teeth were knocked out of my mouth. In retrospect, it was a turning point. I lost the naivety of unconscious trust that we hope will stick to us from babyhood to adulthood. After that, I bounced back. I was an intelligent child. I found academic work easy. I was confident, had friends, and liked my school. I was also gifted with a good singing voice, nurtured by our church choir. I won an award for art. There were a couple of years during my early adolescence when I felt I could do anything I turned my hand to. I just seemed to be on a winning streak. Life felt effortless.

My real love was acting. I loved the ability to read the crowd. Feeling its energy, or lack of it, and being able to play a wannabe-conductor role. I was given the good parts at school, was picked for a couple of children's roles at the English National Opera, got through an audition to be part of the Old Vic Youth Theatre group, run by the before-he-was-famous Griff Rhys Jones. I felt I could connect with people. I wasn't shy. I could look them in the eyes and feel them looking back at me, and felt I could understand something of them. I loved the fluency with which I could speak written words. The ease with which I could step into character. The connection I could forge with an audience.

But there was one problem: my weight, and the way I thought about it.

From a very young age, I ate too much. I ate too much because food tasted so good, so why wouldn't you? I couldn't relate to people who claimed to feel full. Food was about the enjoyment of taste, not about energy requirements. I became self-conscious and developed a poor self-image. 'Too much Coca-Cola,' said the woman who'd come to measure us all at school. My cheeks burned with embarrassment. I wanted to tell her that I didn't drink Coca-Cola, that she was making an assumption and that it was unfair. But that was nothing compared with the growing sense of self-loathing I felt at being labelled fat. This was before I was even ten.

Around the time I knocked my teeth out, I went on a youth hostelling holiday in the Lake District with three friends. One night we stayed in a hostel alongside a whole team of young boys on a school trip. I remember we all slept in a huge room on bunk beds. They started teasing me for being fat, and soon it developed into a sort of chant. All I could think of was *Lord of the Flies*, and Piggy. I felt utter shame.

None of us talked about this. Ever. I did an expert job of refusing to acknowledge the incident, burying it deep. I remembered it only recently, when I started seeing a psychologist, my weight having yo-yoed my entire life.

By the time I was sixteen, the confidence and assurance and ease with which I had achieved my goals were crumbling. It was around this time that my sister Frances left for university. My brother Ben had left home for boarding school when I was ten. Faced with a house empty of siblings, my parents agreed to host a friend's daughter while she went to school in London. The two of us clashed unexpectedly and disastrously. Her idea of a date with a boy was eating at a restaurant. Mine was for me and the boy to commit several illicit acts. She wore clear nail varnish. I wore a donkey jacket.

My acting tailed off. The Old Vic theatre production clashed with the family holiday to Ireland, so I pulled out. The dreaded 'O' levels loomed ever closer. I reached for a smoke, cheerfully in denial, resting on tatty laurels.

I found schoolwork pale in comparison to the attractions of a social life. I couldn't concentrate on it because, well, why would I? I more or less moved into the local pub, the Rose & Crown – or the Rose & Pose as we called it. Sitting endlessly around sipping lager and gin, chatting and staring, flirting and shying away. Everyone watching each other, hiding their forensic ability to judge a person by an invisible barometer of cool measured by a flick of cigarette ash, the bat of an eyelid, the ability to get or give a clever joke laced with irony or sarcasm or some such needle of pain.

It was a libidinous scene, parents playing with each other, divorces erupting and the occasional unexpected pregnancy thrown into the mix. My mum and I watched Andrea Newman's *Bouquet of Barbed Wire* – an ITV series about an incestuous relationship between father and daughter – and thought, Ah, there goes Greenwich.

What were my values, my friends' values? We didn't talk about them much, but you could say that we were more anti than pro. We hated Thatcher but we weren't galvanised behind the left, which was fractured. Music was our political party. It provided our branding, our tribe, our identity. From spiky punk hair to fishnet tights under our old-fashioned school uniform (which included a tie for girls – why?).

I was distracted by all the social shenanigans. A couple of friends stumbled across a dump of 600 Luncheon Vouchers, coupons which companies gave employees as a perk that they could use in restaurants as a form of free business lunches, mysteriously left in a rubbish bin in Blackheath. We delighted in the discovery, seeing ourselves as south-east London's Seventies teenage version of *Bonnie and Clyde* crossed with *The Sting*. We'd sell bunches of LVs for weed, but most of the time we traded the vouchers in for burgers from Wimpy and McDonald's, leading to our ever-expanding girth. We were eventually caught by the police, or rather the boys were. They put on their best white middle-class accents and escaped with a warning. The ringleader won a place at the Royal Academy of Dramatic Art a year later. The LV experience had clearly helped him perfect his craft.

I wandered aimlessly and wittily through a haze of

Benson & Hedges smoke, half a lager and a packet of crisps please, yearning for love and doubting my ability to attract anyone, ever. Full of self-doubt, but happy enough.

Until the day I received my 'O' level results.

I did staggeringly badly. I collapsed in tears, distraught at the chickens marching home to roost, self-disgust and shame hitting me in waves. I wasn't clever, I was stupid. The slip of paper said so. I'd known I wasn't working hard enough, but I had thought I could get through. Because I knew I could think. I knew my brain could make quick connections. I knew I could have ideas. I could memorise lines for a play with ease. But I also knew my mind closed off when it wasn't engaged. My only interest in Latin was why we had to speak in an English accent. Wouldn't it have been more authentic – more fun for that matter – to speak it with an Italian accent? I asked the teacher precisely that question, rousing a giggle from the class, at which point she peered over her glasses and instructed me to focus on the ablative absolute. I still don't know what that is other than a nice bit of alliteration. The RE (religious education) teacher called me a PITN, a Pain In The Neck. Because, I think, I chatted wittily – it seemed to me – pretty much non-stop, and because I would sneak to the toilet for a Benson & Hedges, or occasionally naughtier drugs – nothing really really bad, but certainly bad enough.

Wit, it turned out, was no match for 'O' levels. I went back to school without my donkey jacket which, I found out years later, my mother had hidden. And for the first time in a long while, I knuckled down to homework. I stopped skipping classes for secret ciggies. And I started to enjoy the process of memory in learning, recognising its role in building blocks to greater insights and understanding.

Two years later I applied to Oxbridge. I was accepted to King's College, Cambridge, to read history, the same place where my sister had made a quantum leap in the family's achievements by being awarded a scholarship, also to study history, a few years previously.

Perhaps, I thought, I had crossed a meridian and turned things around.

3

Attitude

From the moment I had my seizure, there was no route for me to psychological relaxation. Distraction was impossible. I couldn't read a book. I could hardly take in a film. I spent most afternoons lying in bed watching mindless shows featuring boring people doing up horrible houses.

I was permanently on my guard. I didn't really feel as though I slept, although of course I must have. The demarcation between sleeping and waking became so blurred that I would start the day unsure whether I'd slept or not. I had thought I might have dreams or nightmares which I should record. I bought myself a notebook to do just that, placing it within easy reach of my bed. It stayed empty. Night after night I had one single thought: that everything had changed in the most unexpected way. Was it really true? Could it really be true?

Feelings of anxiety and confusion started when I left the hospital and were at their most intense between that moment and the start of my treatment. *I am very sick. This is seriously serious, and I am out of all comfort zones.* Those days shook my world. And they were coloured red. The couple of weeks between leaving the hospital and starting radiation were the toughest I've ever experienced. I still didn't know what kind of tumour I had. No one had yet said cancer, and my butchered brain was still processing how the hell I'd gone from walking up a hill to having my head opened up.

I called the surgeon's office. Again and again. 'Hi, it's Jessica Morris here. Would it be possible to have a chat with the surgeon about the pathology – I'm keen to know what kind of tumour I had.' 'Hello, it's Jessica Morris again. Is it possible for me to see the pathology report from my surgery?' 'Hi, me again. I'm sorry I keep calling but I'm anxious to hear the results of the pathology report on my tumour.' What is it about us Brits – or us patients – that makes us apologise all the time?

At last, the surgeon rang me back. I grabbed a paper and pen, and we talked. He sounded upbeat, energetic, fast. He chatted for a while and then told me I had a 'glioma' and that it was quite common. There was something in his tone. I can't remember exactly what he said, but I can picture now, in my handwriting, the word glioma. I knew about a longer word, glioblastoma, which my googling had informed me was the worst kind. I think I didn't ask him if that's what I had because I didn't want to have it.

Instead, I asked: 'Are you telling me I'm out of here?'

'No, no, you're not going anywhere, that's not at all what I meant.'

But what did he mean?

He told me not to google brain tumours. Too late for that. He might as well have told me not to breathe. I knew there are 120 different kinds. What was the difference between a glioma and a glioblastoma? Oh, the peril of additional syllables.

Enter Jenn.

I always loved that game of joining the dots. My father's mother, Nana, taught it to me – how to draw ten dots horizontally and vertically, and then take turns joining dot to dot with a line, creating squares signed with your initials. The winner was the one who made the most squares. I would get lost in the delightful challenge of making rows and columns of tiny dots as near perfectly vertical and horizontal as could be. Sealing each box with a final line was smugly satisfying.

I guess I like networking. Joining a dot to a dot, a thought to a thought, one person to another. I met Jenn through Alicia. I met Alicia through Daniel. I met Daniel through Ed. Ed met Daniel through Clive. Clive and

Yasmin were our neighbours in London. Clive's sister lived in New York.

London, New York, friends, neighbours, all connected.

Jenn is a paediatric oncologist. Scrub that. Jenn is an extraordinarily thoughtful, intelligent, empathetic, loving and persistent person. I didn't know her well, but I had a deep respect for her, and found her intriguing. She'd become pregnant relatively late in life, and had an ambiguous result to her amniocentesis. I was hiking with her and Alicia in upstate New York when she asked us our opinion about her pregnancy. I was struck by the subtlety with which she sought our views and tested hers. All three of us are unashamedly opinionated women. Jenn got what she needed from us in a way that I suspect she replicated with many others, as she sought to weigh the risks associated with the options in front of her. The quiet cleverness of her path to a decision stayed with me. (I'm happy to report that she's now the mother of one of the smartest and most charming boys I've ever met.)

When Jenn heard about my diagnosis she got in touch. Several times. 'Did the surgeon say glioma or glioblastoma?' she asked me. 'I think glioma, but let me check,' I said. Surely it's not the worst? When I open the envelope it's going to say I've done really well, isn't it? I can change the exam grade right up until the moment I see it. Who's to say I can't?

I found my scrap of paper where I'd jotted notes with ballpoint pen while talking to the surgeon. Glioma. Glioma. Not glioblastoma. 'He said "glioma",' I told Jenn.

'Good, that means it could be a number of types.' I clung to that.

I started googling again. I found that glioma refers to brain tumours that develop from glial cells, gluey matter that surrounds and supports neurons and other elements of the nervous system.

Sounded a bit like something out of *Alien*. 'Glioma' is the name for any kind of malignant tumour developing from those cells. Why is a tumour called malignant and not cancer? A small, typical aside that pops into my brain whenever I go medical googling.

So why did he say only that I had a glioma? Why wasn't he more precise?

Then, of course, I realised why. Nobody wants to deliver bad news.

A decade before the Waldorf wobble, Ed asked me a question.

'What would you say if we moved to the States for a few years?'

Be still. Keep a lid on the fear. Oooh ... what's that? Excitement? Yes! Be brave!

I'm from a mafia of Morrises, and I married into an equally powerful family of Pilkingtons. Ed and I are both the youngest of these mighty empires of relatives stuffed with intelligence, achievement, drive and affection. They could be pretty bloody terrifying.

In the blue corner, we have the Morrises, fully paid-up members of the arts team. Father and brother are architects. Mother an artist. Sister possibly the world's finest art curator. In the red, we face off with the Pilkingtons: parents and two siblings are doctors, the other sibling a lawyer.

Professionals, successful, progressive, loving, excellent company. It was comforting to have siblings who'd already been there, who'd forged a path ahead. The choices were clear for us, based on the ones they'd already chosen.

Moving to the United States represented a breakaway. The suspension of decision-making that comes with being the babies of the best is seductive. Ed and I had both benefited from having perhaps a little less focus on our career choices, or at least the perception of a little less. Given that our older siblings were overflowing with personality and achievement, our parents were perhaps less controlling of us than they had been of our elders. They had tested parenting skills on their firstborn, and as a result were much less bothered by the time they got to us. We realised, even intuitively, that this gave us a freedom to choose our own paths, Ed into journalism, me into PR. Both, perhaps, in the world of communication and connectivity.

'What would you say if we moved to the States for a few years?'

It was 2006. I was curled up on the sofa, having finally managed to put the kids to bed. Ed always missed bed-time. His job as UK news editor of *The Guardian* meant he was hardly ever home. He'd gone from writing to editing when our first child, Felix, was a year old. He'd been editing for ten years, first as international news editor, then as UK. Felix would lay a place for his father at the table before he went to bed, including a wine glass which he would insist on filling, even if the only wine available was from the bottle of dregs used for cooking. He knew his father worked a long day, and he adored him. Ed would organise special 'no bye-bye Daddy days' for each child, in the hope of keeping a strong connection with each of them.

With Ed's responsibilities at work increasing, I began to work less. The magic of a day with my son felt so much more important than anything else. I didn't choose to step back as much as I felt compelled to do so. We wanted more children, and I felt an overwhelming desire to be with them. And we were lucky enough to be able to afford it. I had enjoyed my job and was proud of being the first female board director of Fishburn Hedges while working four days a week. The company was a tight-knit professional family of consultants and support staff, where Christmas parties included colleagues' children who made a beeline to reception where they mimicked the receptionist's voice to incoming, bemused callers.

I'd gone freelance/self-employed/set up a small consultancy. Call it whatever. Three days a week, a succession of fabulous au pairs (with some notable exceptions) would take care of our growing brood while I worked. I was surprised and delighted to find that clients walked through the door, mostly as a result of the great contacts and networks I'd made at Fishburn Hedges. I found myself working for heavy hitters, mostly women, at the top of government agencies charged with monitoring and enforcing anti-discrimination legislation relating to women, Black and other diverse communities, and people with disabilities.

And then Ed dropped the big New York question. What to do? I was more than capable of creating a list of reasons not to go, but they couldn't begin to balance with the delicious tingling of excitement I was starting to feel. This wasn't the time for caveats. This was a chance to invest in an adventure and take a risk. I was proud that I could say: 'Yes, let's do it.'

My skin started prickling with nerves. Every time I told someone what we were doing, I buzzed. Their excitement and surprise motivated me further. I found myself describing it as a Willy Wonka golden ticket out of a potential mid-life crisis – we'd completed our family and were happy, but by shaking things up we might avoid what seemed like the inevitable estrangement that comes with middle age. We thought we'd go for a maximum of four years, by which time Felix, our eldest, would be thirteen and good to re-enter the UK education system in time for GCSEs.

We left on 11 August 2006 with seventeen pieces of luggage. We flew the day before the police thwarted a huge plot to smuggle bombs disguised as soft drinks onto transatlantic flights, upending air travel for the rest of the summer. Luck was on our side.

We had had no idea where to live. We had taken a week the previous March to make a tour of the city to check out houses and schools. We decided our criteria were simple: an American public school so the children could make American friends quickly, and ideally a place near a park.

We ended up renting an apartment in a brownstone near Prospect Park in Brooklyn. Over the years, the kids and I walked every square inch of that park. We got to know the lakes, the playgrounds, the swans, the wild area, the merry-go-round, the ice rink. We would head to our friends Stefano and Robyn's favourite tree for picnics. We would lie down on the grass, marvel at the multitude of different trees and leaves and colour, gaze at the gorgeous sky. There were old people, young people, Black people, white people, people drumming, people throwing frisbees, old drunken men sitting in a quiet corner under a tree hidden by the long grass by the lake. Every time we went to the park it felt like a game of pass the parcel: we would peel off another layer of Brooklyn and discover new secrets. It was a never-ending game of discovery, and one which was public, open, owned by all. I could watch my new fellow citizens in a shared space.

I haven't had a dream about Greenwich since we moved.

The job of finally breaking the bad news to me about my diagnosis was passed by the surgeon to a New York neuro-oncologist who, to spare his blushes, I'm going to call Dr Dre (I know, Dr Dre's a rapper, but Felix likes his music). Dr Dre had a glittering résumé. Ed and I shared his online biography and whatever else we could find out about him with our friends and family. None of the many doctors in the Pilkington–Morris gang had direct experience or expertise in neuroscience, but they had bucketloads of medical knowledge, albeit mostly from the British health-care system. Ed and I were looking for reassurance that the man who was in charge of making these critical initial decisions about my healthcare was good at his job. I was putting my life in his hands. We were suitably reassured. Dr Dre's credentials were excellent.

A close friend, Clare, who had been through a terrifying cancer experience and had more than bounced back, agreed to come with me and Ed to the appointment. I wanted to focus solely on what the doctor said and make sure we ran through all the questions we'd prepared in advance, and I wanted Ed to be right there with me in the moment. I knew that Clare would take intelligent notes, make sure we covered everything we wanted to, and generally help us to feel confident in our decision-making.

We were led into a small room. I sat in a large swivel chair, Ed and Clare on smaller chairs against the wall. A smiling nurse practitioner came in and took my pulse, tested my balance, and performed various other routine tests.

Then Dr Dre appeared. He leant against the doorway while confirming my worst fears.

'The pathology report found that your tumour is a glioblastoma.'

I knew it, I knew it, I knew it, I knew it. But also: Don't regret, there's no point.

I was slightly irked that he was standing while I was sitting in this enormous chair; this was clearly going to be a pivotal conversation, and I wanted us to conduct it as equals. But he had a welcome clarity of expression, and soon came across as not only highly intelligent and competent but a really nice guy. When we talked about the side effects of chemotherapy, he likened it to his wife's experience of morning sickness, which I found very reassuring. He had a direct yet gentle gaze, and conveyed a calm authority, matched by his borderline-smart, well-cut and professional-but-not-boring suit.

He then gave me four specific takeaways to hold on

to: that the location of my tumour, its size, my bounce-back from surgery and overall robust health put me in a relatively good position. He recommended I undertake the 'standard of care' – in other words, the course of treatment recommended for anyone diagnosed with glioblastoma. This comprised surgery, if the tumour was operable (check), then six weeks of combined chemotherapy and radiotherapy, followed by a further six months of chemo on a five-day-a-month schedule.

I asked for a prognosis. He said he couldn't, or wouldn't – oh, the difference one letter can make – give me one. The disease was too complex, too heterogeneous, and all the statistics relating to survival were, by definition, related to the past.

We asked about clinical trials, new treatments, whether there was anything else I could do to improve my chances. He thought I should supplement the standard of care in due course, and that we could consider clinical trials 'further down the line'. He explained how a lot would depend on my genetic makeup. The hospital where I was initially treated had sent a sample of my tumour to be analysed, and the results would show if I had any genetic mutations that might suit particular trials, or treatments used to treat other cancers. I realised I was now part of the dawn of 'personalised medicine'.

But I am no fool. As he spoke, I could hear myself respond internally. How can one be in a 'relatively good position' with a disease that has a median survival rate of fourteen months? A less than 5 per cent chance of surviving five years? There's nothing remotely good, let alone relatively good, about that. There's only an overflowing barrel of bad.

Before we left, I asked to go to the bathroom. I had to take a moment for myself, to escape from it all. It was instinctive. I had finally, after days of waiting, been delivered an overwhelming diagnosis – glioblastoma – and I couldn't cope with the reality of it. This was final confirmation of what had been a dawning reality. This was it. There was no going back from it.

In the bathroom there was a mirror straight in front of me. I needed to stare into it. To stare at my face. To face it – the confirmation of my worst fears. The mirror was big and brand new, so new that it still had sealant around the glass. I noted that the sealant was already peeling. I wondered whether it would need to be fixed quite soon. How long could I stay in the bathroom? I didn't want to leave. I just wanted to look at myself in the mirror and acknowledge what was happening to me while simultaneously running away. I thought about people whose lives change irrevocably and irreversibly. Now I was one of that club. The Irrevocable Irreversible Moment Club.

Glioblastoma. The worst of all 120-plus different forms of brain tumour. Dre had talked about radiotherapy, chemotherapy, recurrence. He'd confirmed my worst suspicions. Glioblastoma. In a nanosecond, my life had gone from one of smooth, predictable joy to one of unimaginable terror. Glioblastoma.

Death. Soon. Everything over. No future. No seeing my children become adults. No grandchildren. No fulfilment of potential. No dreams. No cure. Glioblastoma.

GLIOBLASTOMA.

I felt a sober strength running through me. It wasn't just a question of whether I could cope with these treatments. Or whether I could even accept such an extraordinary change in my life. It was a recognition that my relationship with this disease was, fundamentally, down to me. That I alone had this unique version of it, and I alone could choose to take the helm. No one was going to know what it was like to be me. The question staring back at me in the mirror was whether I understood this and whether I chose to engage. The mirror was like a test of myself. I was in genuinely new territory, I'd just learned that my life was about to end. No clever doctors, medicines, family or friends would get me through this without me consciously, and continuously, going at it. Being alone with my disease was a reality – my choice was whether to see that as an opportunity I could bet on meeting, or whether I would allow its intrinsic terror to overwhelm me. I could look in the mirror, take some time for myself. Look at and into myself. Take in my reflection. Tiny details suddenly became terribly important. The peeling sealant around the mirror. Think about that to avoid the terror. My life was ending. Think about the sealant. I stared into the mirror, a proxy of my poor bruised self, and waited for my psyche to answer. And then it was there, like a high-speed juggernaut come to rest at so gentle a pace the passengers couldn't even feel it. Yes. I was up to the task ahead. I was and am and will be strong. I chose to take this on.

My seizure had been so shocking and so public that our friends and family all heard about it straight away. The outpouring of concern and support was extraordinary. Everyone wanted to help. We were inundated with beautiful gifts of flowers, food, cakes. Ed was keeping people up to date with what was happening, even though we really had no idea ourselves. Our email chain of people to update was getting longer and longer, and it was becoming quite difficult to keep up with it. Wesley and Jill, two of our closest friends, got together and suggested they set up a blog. It meant we just had to send one email to everyone, and was a huge relief.

Ed began the updating, but quite soon I found myself wanting to assert my voice. I railed against being the passive victim of an evil stranger in my head. Telling people in my own words was one way of pretending I had a little bit of control over this monster.

9 February 2016 10:42 pm

FIRST TRIP TO THE DOCTOR

We saw Dr Dre, the neuro-oncologist I've been referred to, today. He has proposed aggressive treatment for the aggressive tumour I have been confirmed to have. That involves six weeks of radiation and chemo (in the form of pills) combined – the radiation five days a week and the chemo every day. Then a second stage of chemo alone lasting six months.

He said that people's experiences of the treatment vary enormously. In the first stage, which should start in about a week, some people can feel incredibly tired, others not so. So we'll see, and deal with whatever comes at us.

Dr Dre is obviously at the forefront of new experimental techniques which are based on each individual's genetic makeup, and are customised to them alone. He made clear to us that he would put my needs first, and would make sure I got onto any clinical trial that was appropriate for me. He stressed that this world is moving incredibly rapidly, with innovations coming thick and fast. But he also emphasised that clinical trials tend to take place further down the road, after the more conventional round of radiation and chemo is over. And only then if needed. So again, we'll see.

He came up with four reasons to be cheerful: the tumour was small; most of it was taken out in surgery; it is in a relatively 'silent' part of the brain where damage to functions is less likely; and my age which should make me more resilient to the side effects of treatment. Beyond that he underlined the importance of exercise and a healthy diet, so I'm going to be walking regularly in Prospect Park – companions more than welcome please! – and with Tess and Emma now declared vegans that should make sure my diet is from now on suitably austere. Yug.

Dr Dre has advised that I will need to be accompanied every day to radiotherapy, which I've opted to have done at NYU because it's easy to get to from our house. The treatment should start in about a week or so. We were so impressed by Dr Dre that we expect to stick with him.

That's it for now.

Choosing Doctors

Jenn called. She listened carefully to my account of the meeting. She suggested we seek a second opinion, from a centre with a greater research capability. It made sense. Now that I knew I had a disease with no cure, I wanted to be treated by wannabe Nobel laureates who saw cracking glioblastoma – and saving my life in the process – as major motivators.

She introduced me to her colleague, Fabio Iwamoto, deputy director of neuro-oncology at Columbia University. He met me, Ed and Clare in his office at 51st Street. He shook my hand and we sat down. A pile of papers was neatly arranged on his desk. He looked me calmly in the eye and asked how I was. He was a slight, nattily dressed guy. I was intrigued by his name. He spoke quietly as he examined my strength and balance. I liked that he hadn't delegated this ritual to a nurse, but had touched the sick one himself.

Dr Iwamoto explained that the results of following the 'standard of care' were 'sub-optimal'. I came to hate that phrase, 'sub-optimal'. It was such an understatement that I felt it to be almost offensive, even while I understood that some patients might find it helpful in coming to terms with the overwhelming diagnosis of glioblastoma. My interpretation of the phrase 'sub-optimal' was 'it doesn't work'. In the vast majority of cases like mine, the standard of care doesn't work. Which makes 'sub-optimal' more than an understatement – it's a euphemism for the grim reaper.

He then showed me the printouts of five clinical trials and experimental treatments on his desk.

We ran through the clinical trial options, which were pretty thin and disappointing. None of them suggested we might be on the brink of a cure. We settled on what was then an unproven form of immunotherapy for glioblastoma. Nivolumab, or 'Opdivo', is a checkpoint inhibitor. That means it removes the cunning barrier that cancer cells place on the captains in our immune systems, which then prohibits the soldiers from following their natural instinct, which is of course to kick out foreign enemies like my glioblastoma cells.

Nivolumab hadn't – and still hasn't – been shown to be sufficiently successful to become part of the standard of care. But Dr Iwamoto had around twenty patients taking it on the drug company's compassionate use programme. Side effects seemed minimal. I signed up.

Dr Iwamoto was keen that I get a couple of doses in during the six weeks of radiation and chemo I was about to start. He explained there was increasing interest in the potential synergy of taking these treatments together.

I found myself drawn to this. I liked the idea of synergies. Not looking at one treatment in isolation. Google kept emphasising the complexity of the disease, so why would a 'one size fits all' treatment work anyhow? I needed a crash course in cancer.

We went back to Dr Dre for his view. He thought immunotherapy would be something to look at further down the line. If we were to introduce it alongside radiotherapy and chemo, we would risk setting the immunotherapy up to fail, because my immune system would be compromised by all the treatments, especially the chemotherapy which suppresses the body's immune system.

Ed and I wanted to talk to Dre and Iwamoto together in a four-way conference to discuss whether to add in nivolumab or not. I just assumed this would be the most sensible and efficient way to agree what would be best for me, the patient. How naive can you be? It became clear that getting us all together round the table, physically or virtually, was not going to be easy. It was more complicated than we had realised. They were busy doctors and, while generous with their time, it seemed really difficult to set up a joint call.

We were in such a state that it never occurred to us that the doctors would not be delighted to have an open discussion with us. Together. Here were two scientists, both world leaders in their highly specialised field, to some degree at odds with each other in terms of the advice they were giving me, but apparently reluctant to talk to me together about their different approaches. This puzzled me. I was ready to make a difficult choice, but it didn't seem sensible for the doctors to treat this complex disease in isolation from each other. Surely each was more interested in helping the patient discuss which one to go for? Surely the best way for them to do that was to have a joint discussion and debate? But I couldn't make it happen.

So choosing which path to take was going to fall to me

and Ed. To say that it was a critical decision is another spectacular understatement. I was confident that each of these doctors was exemplary. They were both at the top of their game. But I had to take it all on trust. One was saying go with this new treatment with relatively slim evidence that it works, but that, in my situation, some evidence was better than none; the other was saying it would be counterproductive to introduce an immunotherapy drug when my body was under strain from chemotherapy, and that it could complicate finding new treatments later. They each based their advice, conflicting as it was, on deep knowledge of the genetic makeup and functioning of the brain. You can't get that stuff on Google, hard as I tried to find it. It was based on global scientific understanding, umpteen peer-reviewed papers, years of clinical research – and here I was, a civilian, being asked to judge a beauty contest between the two.

And it was a contest in which the stakes were incredibly high. Later, I came to understand what had happened. From the perspective of the doctors, their advice could be taken or rejected. They had never met me before. Their understanding was clinical rather than personal. But this was the most important decision of my life. The idea that I would have to make the call over and above world-leading scientists, despite my complete lack of knowledge, was actually less stupid than it sounded to me at the time.

How was I to make the decision? It couldn't be on the

basis of genetic pathways or mutations – I knew nothing about that. Instead, it would come down to my sense of who I was and what I wanted. I was attracted to the idea of taking the more aggressive approach, the one that had the promise of something new. I don't see myself as a 'standard of care' person. I was more afraid of being complacent and doing the regular thing than of trying something entirely unproven, however risky.

I contacted a friend, Barak Goodman, a film producer behind the PBS version of Siddhartha Mukherjee's book *The Emperor of All Maladies: A Biography of Cancer*, and took him up on the offer of help he'd made when I was diagnosed. I knew Barak from mutual friends and had once talked to him about what was then the beginnings of his documentary series. I had been impressed by his enthusiasm for the project. For me, at that point, cancer was an intriguing disease; I had thought it must be a fascinating project to work on. Now, cancer was far more than intriguing. Barak's work had real personal urgency.

I called him on a Sunday morning. I asked him if he could suggest anyone I could talk to who might be able to advise me on which route to choose – standard of care versus an unproven experimental treatment? Barak said he'd talked to a neuro-oncologist named Dr Michael Lim who was then at Johns Hopkins Hospital (he's now at Stanford); Barak had been very impressed by Dr Lim's confidence in the potential of immunotherapy treatment for glioblastoma. He immediately put us in touch, and thirty minutes later Lim rang me back. I was stunned when I picked up the phone and realised who was on the line. Here I was talking to yet another world-leading scientist. Terrified at the speed of his response, and awed by this big brain talking to unprepared me, I scrambled to marshal my thoughts. I explained my dilemma. I asked him: 'What would you do if you were me?' He paused before saying he thought that what Dr Iwamoto was proposing was 'not unreasonable'. I took that to mean that there was a chance that immunotherapy might work, but no guarantees.

I called Dr Dre to explain that I was taking the other, more experimental route, and to thank him. I moved to Columbia and started infusions of the immunotherapy drug soon after.

I was relieved. A decision had been made. I felt it was my decision – with a little bit of world-class counsel – but I did wish that I had been able to bring both those doctors together. It didn't feel right to have two amazing physicians with my best interest at heart who were nevertheless unable to work together to forge the best solution for me. A joint decision, a collective one, would have been the best thing for me, and I was the patient. I wanted to say to them that if they truly wanted what was best for me, if they could fully embrace my question, 'What would you do if you were me?', they could have set aside their individual professional positions, put the patient first, and worked towards a joint resolution.

At least I wasn't powerless in the decision. I was in the enviable position of being able to exercise choice, and I was able to do that because I was a patient. This was the first time in my journey that I was in a position of power, and feeling strong enough to make difficult decisions that might change the course of my disease. In deciding to go with Dr Iwamoto, who rapidly became Fabio to me, I had demonstrated that I was brave enough to take on an unproven therapy. To do something different, caution be damned. Risk-taking had never felt so good.

17 February 2016 10:57 pm

DECISION TIME

Treatment with Dr Iwamoto at Columbia starts on Tuesday next week. I've been quiet on this site because me and Ed have been working round the clock since I last wrote, trying to figure out which treatment option and which doctor to go with. It's been a record-breaking, rapid and vertical learning line in highly complex medical, moral and wtf learning. We've gone with Dr Iwamoto because he has suggested adding in an immunotherapy treatment alongside radiotherapy and chemotherapy from the start. It's the drug that's behind the turnaround success treatment for people with melanoma. This is really early days for doing this for what I have, and there is not one bit of data to indicate whether it will work. But there's enough medical rationale from people far above my intelligence grade, plus basic logic (fight aggressive cancer with aggression; hit the cells when they're dazed after surgery; adding in another agent might help). But thanks to our tentacles of connections, combined PR/media tenacity, and overriding hunger to do our utmost to wash this mass right out of my head (as the song really should go), I'm confident in the decision we've made.

In other headlines ... I tested positive for a gene that is proven to improve outcomes with the chemo. Small but important yay. And I spent the best part of two hours in various donut machines having MRIs on Monday – where is my MRI survivor Oscar??

Tomorrow I swear I will sort the calendar and organise all the fabulous and extraordinary heart-warming offers of help. But now, the lure of Netflix is calling yet again ... Thank you my fabulous friends, and more soon.

4

Embracing the Madness

Your Attention Please

by Peter Porter

The Polar DEW has just warned that
A nuclear rocket strike of
At least one thousand megatons
Has been launched by the enemy
Directly at our major cities.
This announcement will take
Two and a quarter minutes to make,
You therefore have a further
Eight and a quarter minutes
To comply with the shelter

Requirements published in the Civil
Defence Code – section Atomic Attack.
A specially shortened Mass
Will be broadcast at the end
Of this announcement –
Protestant and Jewish services
Will begin simultaneously –
Select your wavelength immediately
According to instructions
In the Defence Code. Do not
Take well-loved pets (including birds)
Into your shelter – they will consume
Fresh air. Leave the old and bed-
ridden, you can do nothing for them.
Remember to press the sealing
Switch when everyone is in
The shelter. Set the radiation
Aerial, turn on the geiger barometer.
Turn off your television now.
Turn off your radio immediately
The Services end. At the same time
Secure explosion plugs in the ears
Of each member of your family. Take
Down your plasma flasks. Give your children
The pills marked one and two
In the C.D. green container, then put
Them to bed. Do not break

The inside airlock seals until
The radiation All Clear shows
(Watch for the cuckoo in your
perspex panel), or your District
Touring Doctor rings your bell.
If before this, your air becomes
Exhausted or if any of your family
Is critically injured, administer
The capsules marked 'Valley Forge'
(Red pocket in No. 1 Survival Kit)
For painless death. (Catholics
Will have been instructed by their priests
What to do in this eventuality.)
This announcement is ending. Our President
Has already given orders for
Massive retaliation – it will be
Decisive. Some of us may die.
Remember, statistically
It is not likely to be you.
All flags are flying fully dressed
On Government buildings – the sun is shining.
Death is the least we have to fear.
We are all in the hands of God,
Whatever happens happens by His Will.
Now go quickly to your shelters.

My sister and I were obsessed with this poem. We wallowed in the feeling of perpetual doom. We were Seventies kids. *Silent Spring* was one of our bibles. I read *The Death of Grass* over and over. Frances's school project was on air pollution. A few years later, my art 'A' level was similarly themed. We spent hours with Rotring pens cross-hatching plumes of smoke. We drove to and from Ireland twice a year, and even as I type this today I can smell the pollution from the power stations on the way to the Swansea docks and the ferry to smoggy Ireland.

'Your Attention Please' represented our apocalyptic fear, whether it was the Seventies oil crisis, or the three-day week, or the advent of Cruise missiles. There was one particularly bleak family holiday when we read it incessantly. We were a sailing family. My mother's father and brother were in the Navy. My father grew up in Bournemouth, learning to sail before he could swim. Even before he had learnt to speak properly, my father used to harangue his mother to 'wee the wee' – his infant attempt to say 'see the sea'. He had to see it, feel it and sail it. And on a sunny day with a brisk breeze, sailing a dinghy through blue waters is hard to beat.

But this particular family holiday saw no sun, just grey waters and cold rain, as we tacked our way through a nondescript stretch of the Thames estuary. When the wind rose, my father and brother took charge, my sister, mother and I slinking down into the cabin, pulling the hatch down, and indulging in macabre irony. We read Peter Porter's poem out loud, in voices that sounded like wartime tannoys. We play-acted the end of the world. We couldn't go on deck because of the risk of radiation. When we got to shore, we would find a devastated world full of relics of the nuclear apocalypse that we decided had occurred while we were on the water. We would find misshapen stones and marvel at them as pieces of London Bridge, shattered by 'the bomb', leaving its detritus scattered. When we finally got home to Greenwich, we would have to scrub and scrub to get rid of all the radiation poisoning.

I guess it was good prep for a later reality.

23 February 2016 5:20 pm

DAY 1 OF TREATMENT

Twenty-nine days left. I completed my first radiotherapy session today. It was a breeze. Much, much easier than expected. The horrid bit is being pinned down with a mask moulded to my face. No way to open eyes or mouth yuk. The good bit is you can connect your phone to the sound system. My man Stevie and his Golden Lady, from *Innervisions* (back in the day), got me through in no time.

I was expecting the opposite. When I had the mask fitted last week, it felt like eternity. Lying still, in silence and darkness, with no sense of time passing. So I had a spontaneous visualisation: there I was, in one of Felix's Xbox games, set inside my brain. Facing me were lots of tunnels, representing the different pathways in my brain. Inside the tunnels were grey, faceless soldiers – just like those plastic toy soldiers kids have. I lay there and zapped the buggers. Each time I moved onto a new tunnel, I turned quickly back to zap one that had sneakily hidden. And once I was 200 per cent sure I'd cleared a tunnel, I painted it in a special super-strong paint to ensure the soldiers could never, ever come back. I knew I'd feel OK about letting Felix have *COD* (*Call of Duty*) one day.

I have to do a total of thirty radiotherapy sessions spread over six weeks. Ed came with me and got me to draw a thick black line through today's session on my appointment sheet. Mmm.

Tonight I take my first anti-nausea pill, followed by chemo pills. The theory is you sleep through the worst. You have to take them with a large glass of water. The kindly nurse said I may have to visit the bathroom in the night. I explained my gender and age and said this was where the benefit of life experience might come in.

Dr Iwamoto's office is working on the funding for

the immunotherapy. We hope to add that in next week and I'll take it intravenously, fortnightly. (Which, my Yankee friends, is a useful word that for some inexplicable reason didn't seem to make it through customs from The Other Side.)

Thank you for the delicious meals that are being delivered. And all the volunteers to accompany me to and from radiotherapy. And all the other crazy, wonderful and life-affirming support y'all are giving me. I'm thinking of going one better than Cindy Adams, the gossip columnist with her famous pay-off line 'Only in New York, kids, only in New York'. My version will be: Only in Park Slope, people, only in Park Slope.

X

I started to wrestle with writing down what was happening for my friends. I have written for work for years. But now I felt a compulsion and desire to communicate what I was feeling. I wanted to take the people I love with me, so I would feel less alone. It was a managed form of communication; these early blog posts gave me an unexpected strength. I was surprised how liberating it was writing in my voice and at my pace. My friends were complimentary about my posts, which encouraged me to go further. The more encouragement I received, the more writing I produced, and the more insights I derived from the writing itself. Of course I now see this was a form of therapy. I derived strength from being able to articulate what I was feeling, and that in itself felt empowering. I started to blog furiously.

How do you tell your children who are just at the edge of adulthood that everything is going to change, that all the certainties and assumptions you brought them up with without even realising have suddenly vanished, and that you are just as ignorant as they are? How do you deliver awful news when your job as a parent is always to protect your children from dark things?

When I had the seizure on the hillside Felix was eighteen, Tess sixteen and Emma thirteen. For them the early days of my diagnosis were very intense, full of drama and people and food being brought round, gifts arriving at the door. There was an element of never-ending party to it that was strangely cheerful amid what they could divine was bad news. We had to make sure that they knew how serious this was, without making them so terrified it could knock them off course. We decided we would sit them down and talk to them. With so many other people around, we wanted to make it slightly formal, all in the same room and round the table. We wanted to be connected to them without scaring them.

Ed began the conversation. He said that I was unwell and that it was serious. We had a very good medical team, he went on, and we were in New York where the best medical teams are, and that was a very good thing. I followed up by saying I had a brain tumour. Felix said, 'Well that sucks.' That pretty much summed it up, I thought. Tess was silent in a way that meant she was processing what I was saying. Emma asked if this meant that I had cancer. Until then, the C-word hadn't been used. Intellectually, I knew it was cancer, but I was having a hard time saying the word. So I said, 'Yes, I think so.' They seemed okay. It felt to me like one of those conversations you are always going to remember – there was no going back from it. It made the diagnosis real, and I felt deeply sad that my children had to know this about their mother.

I remember Tess saying how pleased she was to have me home. She confessed to me that when I was out at work every day, she would wait for me to get back home before starting her homework. Now she had me around much more. That was an unexpected benefit. And the kids could see that outwardly I was fine.

We had thought a lot about whether we would use the word 'glioblastoma' – or GBM, as it's known – such a terrible word with such terrible statistics attached to it. Any reference to GBM online mentions its awful median survival rate, how it is terminal or even that it is an imminent death sentence, with never any word of more positive outcomes or progress in the science. So we decided to avoid it. We didn't censor it so much as deploy alternatives, like 'brain tumour'. That was for us, I can see now, as much as it was for the kids.

Darling,

It is frustrating that you're not allowed to go to radiotherapy on your own. You feel as though you're asking a lot of friends to accompany you, but the doctor is adamant you must have a chaperone. Is that what's going to happen now, for everything? Will you become so disabled that you can't get on the subway and then walk a few blocks all on your own? Why does that feel more depressing than embarking on serious brain zapping?

The good thing is you get one-to-one time with many friends you rarely get to see. You can march from 34th Street to 1st Avenue and catch up.

I know you can't even think about the chemo. At least it's just pills. Maybe you'll get thin – YEAH! Oh Ms Sophisticated, equating diet success with beating cancer. Trite to the end.

Just get on with it.

Jx

29 February 2016 9:27 pm

MR JAGGER JOINS THE TEAM

A good conversation with a doctor when you have a horrible condition is one where he says: 'You are in the best possible state at the moment.'

Five days into radio- and chemotherapy, and that's what Dr Silverman at NYU said to me today. He showed me images of my brain and the area where the tumour was. The surgery I had was pretty much a total resection of the tumour. Latest MRIs show no growth. The two hours in donut machines last week were worth it.

I haven't experienced any side effects as yet. But I'm under no illusions – exhaustion and nausea and all sorts of unspeakable things that require much time in the bathroom are likely to hit midway through treatment.

I'm home now, sitting at the kitchen table while friends and family cook up another amazing feast. I'm feeling happy. Today's meeting was just so good, coming after a weekend when I was down. I'd entered the online patient support community, and came away feeling it should have its own health warning attached.

We are still waiting for the funding for the immunotherapy, hoping to have a first infusion at the end of this week or early next.

And now there's another treatment to add in. This would start after radiotherapy, and it works by creating electric fields that slow and stop cancer cells from dividing. A trial to see if this was effective for people newly diagnosed with the kind of brain tumour I have was stopped at the end of last year because the results were so good. It will take nine months and require a lot of hats, headscarves, wigs, but I'll be able to live normally.

Today I chose to burn through *Gimme Shelter* as my men – two wonderful radiotherapists called Chris and Schmidt – zapped those outrageous invaders. It's just a shot away ... but a much bigger shot at the moment than it might have been.

That first week of radiotherapy a package arrived from the UK. Inside it was a white envelope with the handwritten note: 'We didn't choose these tracks, they chose us'. Inside the envelope was an iPod, with a playlist of Eighties hits we'd grooved to in the Late Night Bar at King's. Harry, now a leading geneticist, had compiled the playlist with Jimmy, now Professor James Doyle at Harvard. Back in the day they were key members of our little band. It only existed for a few months, but we had many a giggle over what to name the group. 'Foolishly' was my favourite, but we settled for 'Jimmy and the Long Drinks'. Jimmy played the piano, smoked B&H and drank too many bottles of Beck's. I sang, not very well, to his piano playing. Harry played the drums, in a skirt, I may add – years before Beckham. And Emma Lilly sang the second verse of 'The Girl from Ipanema' in Portuguese. Our only outing was at an event at King's to raise money for the miners' strike. Ah, if only *The X Factor* had been around then ... Simon Cowell's loss was Harvard's gain.

8 March 2016 6:40 pm

YOU KNOW WHAT

I'm overwhelmed.

Every day I wake up to beautifully crafted, heartfelt and extraordinarily loving messages. I draw great strength from these. But I'm overwhelmed and can't keep pace. Too many years in consultancy, plus very good parenting from the very best parents, mean I can't cope with being slow and bland with replies.

I know you know that, but I want to state on the record that I'm sorry.

It's all the fault of TEF. That's the name my great pal Julia and I have conjured up for the dying mass inside. The Evil Fucker.

The grey faceless soldiers have been replaced with the sun. Weather Report's *Birdland* and *All That Jazz* lead me to see a red target when I close my eyes under the mask. We all see it under the real sun. And for me it's burning away, every day, at 1 pm ET. And it's doing what the sun does, giving life to me. All hail.

Enough of my incoherence. I only want instrumental music under the mask at the mo, while I eat words when freed. My very dear friend Alex Harvey is gifting me a poem daily on Facebook. Each is providing sustenance to a place in my head and my heart that TEF cannot even get a temporary visa for. But this is my favourite so far. It's 'Snow' by Louis MacNeice:

Snow

The room was suddenly rich and the great bay-
window was
Spawning snow and pink roses against it
Soundlessly collateral and incompatible:

World is suddener than we fancy it.
World is crazier and more of it than we think,
Incorrigibly plural. I peel and portion
A tangerine and spit the pips and feel
The drunkenness of things being various.

And the fire flames with a bubbling
sound for world
Is more spiteful and gay than one supposes –
On the tongue on the eyes on the ears in the
palms of one's hands –
There is more than glass between the snow
and the huge roses.

TEF can't match poetry.

PS. Still feeling fine, still waiting for funding, still patient, and still being a good(ish) patient.

X

Looking back, I realise that I had spaced these blogs so I was producing one a week. I was still being inundated with messages from friends, and the blogs helped give some structure to my thoughts. I found myself keeping the tone of the blog posts quite light. Obviously that was as much for me as for my friends and family.

One day a package arrived from a friend, Anne. Inside the bubble wrap was a pair of Weebles. They were pretty ancient but they brought back the childhood games I used to enjoy. I could hear the advertising jingle from the Seventies. I smiled. I tapped the Weeble, watched it wobble, and saw it inexorably stand back up straight. They still sit on our mantelpiece wobbling away and staying upright. Weebles wobble but they don't fall down.

15 March 2016 9:17 am

IN THE BULLRING

My metaphor madness continues. I've been increasingly obsessed with getting to know my enemy, aka

TEF. As we all know, it's a frighteningly intelligent, tough and complex foe. That's one of the main reasons I plumped for a strategy of throwing as many weapons as I could at it as early as possible, rather than rely on the standard of treatment for my kind of brain tumour.

So I'm now a matador, playing a psychological game of engagement and warfare with an enemy that is as keen to win as I am. I got some new ammo last week, with funding secured for the immunotherapy treatment as well as the electrode therapy.

I had my first infusion of immunotherapy on Friday. It was all plain sailing until right at the end, when I had a slight allergic reaction which saw my chest tightening and caused much coughing. Nothing a shot of Benadryl couldn't sort. I'll be having infusions of nivolumab every two weeks from now on.

Electrode therapy – rather confusingly marketed as Optune – will start in May, allowing my sore and increasingly hairless scalp time to recover from radiotherapy.

So I'm all set. A full array of 'banderillas' that I and the army of charming medics helping me are throwing at TEF. The plan is to wound it, lengthening the time I have as more banderillas come on to the market – including the sword thrust, or 'estocada', I'll have great pleasure in plunging into TEF during our final dance.

I miss London and my fabulous family and friends very much. Your emails, photos, gifts, messages, and now even visits, are hugely welcome. My sister – all hail to the new director of Tate Modern! – is with me this week. Many years ago she asked me to cut her hair, while I was staying with her at Cambridge. I gave her what I thought was a very chic short cut. It's taken thirty-seven years for her to return the favour. My hair started falling out last week, and having clumps of over-dyed tresses fall out all over the place is really not nice. Last night Frances snipped away and hey presto, twins we are again. She even said I looked like the scary lady from *House of Cards*. Sibling love can be very blind at times.

All this is good. As was my weekly meeting with Dr Silverman, the super-hero managing my radiotherapy. I'm exactly halfway through the initial six-week radio and chemo programme. Check out Ed's pix to see me and my mask. I asked Silverman to tell me to stop googling, as it tends to bring me down ... and yet I'm drawn irresistibly to researching more aspects of my disease. He paused. Then explained that because I'm unusually young to have this condition, I'm in much better shape than the majority of people he sees. My body is able to tolerate the treatment (apart from an ongoing cold, I really do feel fine), and this, together with the other positive points I have (size and location of tumour, excellent surgery, no regrowth to date), means I have every reason to feel good.

And I do.

X

My blogging was a shield. It helped me to control what I wanted to say but not what I needed to say. I actually didn't know what I needed to say, and I suppose if I'm honest I still don't. Aren't we all searching for those kinds of answers?

Rereading my blogs, I'm struck by how I wanted to be open and share, but I think I found it very hard not to include moments of humour, however warped. Who am I trying to kid? I remember seeking out friends to go with me to radiotherapy whom I knew would adopt a similarly light tone, avoiding heavy empathy. I wasn't denying what was happening, but the ability to crack a joke became increasingly helpful, a prop to lean on.

What I didn't tell my friends and family was that whenever I went for a zapping, I noticed that the other patients around me looked very sick. Most were older than me, none of them was smiling, and no one would meet my gaze. Usually they were accompanied by somebody giving them assistance. It made me terribly sad. I didn't want to be in that room, but I had to be. There was no escape from it.

I found it difficult to share these darker experiences with a wider group. A friend said that I had five years until all the children would be at college, and that if I could just get through to that point, they would be okay. That was supposed to be a positive way of looking at it, and the advice was very lovingly given. But I couldn't help thinking, is that my life horizon now? A few years? Is that all I've got?

21 March 2016 8:05 pm

10, 9, 8 ...

Ten treatments to go. As I twiddle my toes to Youssou N'Dour and Neneh Cherry singing '7 Seconds' ... so many numbers, digits, forms ...

Life doesn't get much more dramatic (I hope) than brain cancer. But there is a side to it which is really, really boring. Endless forms to fill out. Pills to take. Meetings to be had. All of which involve waiting. My whole day seems taken up with that bloody subway ride. The march from 34th and 6th down to 1st Avenue. Turn left at reception. Follow the blue line. Be amazed by the harpist/violinist/guitarist playing in the waiting area of a Monday. Suppress memory of waiting eleven hours at the Whittington for Ed to be X-rayed when he'd been stabbed in 1987, not a nurse in sight, let alone a harpist. Catch elevator to second floor. Time my steps carefully so I don't have to pause while my hand triggers the hand sanitiser to drop its load. Rub in while turning right for radiology, pressing the big button that opens the door for me (wait, am I now counteracting the hand sanitiser by picking up germs?). Say hi to Natalie at reception; admire her yet-another-new-hairstyle. Place hand on space-age palm reader. Suppress repetition of thought of counteracting hand sanitiser on grounds of really too dull. Wait for my guys. Duh, all the technicians are men and all the nurses are women. Check which of Harry's songs on my bespoke Apple shuffle I want to hear today. Jump on gurney, place head for helmet. Twiddle toes. Get outta there.

TG for my mates, accompanying me on this journey every day. And TG there are only ten sessions left.

I'm a bit more tired, a bit more chesty. Or is that because I keep being told that's what I'll feel? I'm certainly more bald. Rather dramatically. From the front I have a fabulous fringe (much as I love this fine country, bangs for a fringe seems a poor swap), but from the back it's like some UFO has landed and burnt a huge crop circle. There's a fringe left at the bottom. A sort of mullet. Nice, eh?

I need to wrap this treatment, get back to work, and get what brain is left back working on things more meaningful than how to describe my hair. And I need to see a therapist.

More soon

X

Each conversation I had with a friend as I marched through Manhattan on my way to radiotherapy helped me reflect on what I was going through. It was like a concentrated injection of therapy, every morning. Because I had always assumed I had good health, I was completely shocked that I was suddenly so unhealthy. So, like other people with this diagnosis, I was looking for things I could do to improve my lot from the get-go. Goodbye to wine, goodbye to carefree eating and drinking. That much was obvious. The doctors had little advice about what alternative or complementary treatments I might try on top of the medical treatments I was receiving. They weren't uniformly against the idea of me experimenting with diets and vitamin supplements, but they were uniformly anxious that I was aware that there was no panacea.

29 March 2016 8:37 pm

JESSICA IS AWAKE

I know this is deeply politically incorrect, and many people suffer terribly from chemo nausea, making it hard for them to eat.

But I do think it unfair that this one side effect which could have led to me emerging from this intensive treatment with an actual bonus – fantasies of a Jessica Morris morphing into Keri Russell kind of thing – has been denied.

The concrete bunker super-factory known as my stomach is very much alive and, as has been the case since 1963, has a seemingly insatiable appetite. Luckily friends continue to deliver the most fabulous feasts. It's not all bad, though. I'm a sugar-free zone, as TEF is apparently magnetically attracted to all things glucose, which works as a super-food, enabling TEF to grow. Same with me, which is all the more reason to steer well clear. But once a week I go further, and fast. It seems TEF is clever, but not that clever. Twelve hours into a fast it gets confused at the change in routine. I picture it sitting around, complaining 'where's my dinner?' and feeling all at odds. Which is exactly why fasting is good, as while TEF is wondering where the next delivery's coming from, it's distracted from its normal evil wrong-doing activity, i.e., causing trouble for me.

I'm lucky to have dodged the nausea bullet (for now). But not so sleep. This other, much trailed side effect from radiotherapy has now kicked in. I return from daily zapping to dissolve into afternoons of Cornish clotted-cream consistency sleeps. A rare moment of wisdom saw me arrange to have our bedroom decorated just before treatment started. It is no longer the bedroom. Not even a master bedroom. It is now a zen retreat of triple Michelin-star marvellousness. Fluffy duvets, fur throws, cashmere blankets ... Couldn't be more perfect.

I really have very little to say other than – all is good, roll on end of zapping (Monday next week), next immunotherapy infusion (Tuesday next week) and then more pills, more medics, and the mad electrodes. I'm doing good. I don't know why I feel happy, but I do. I was struck by Decca Aitkenhead's extraordinary piece in *The Guardian* a few days ago, where she described her partner's death and her treatment for aggressive breast cancer. This leapt out at me: 'When Tony died, no one knew what to say. When I told people I had cancer, everyone knew what I should do ... Above all – and under the circumstances, this one felt like a tall order – it was imperative to Think Positive. We all want to believe there is a cure for bad luck.'

The same day I read this, my addictive googling took me to the writings of Stephen Jay Gould, palaeontologist and educator at Harvard University whose essay 'The Median Isn't the Message' rewrote the rule book on how to interpret statistics. Stephen lived with cancer for many years before dying in 2002. He wrote: 'Attitude clearly matters in fighting cancer. We don't know why (from my old-style materialistic perspective, I suspect that mental states feed back upon the immune system). But match people with the same cancer for age, class, health, socioeconomic status, and, in general, those with positive attitudes, with a strong will and purpose for living, with commitment to struggle, with an active response to aiding their own treatment and not just a passive acceptance of anything doctors say, tend to live longer.'

What I love about this is not just that it blesses one of my few, genetic pluses – my 'Weebles wobble, but they don't fall down' disposition – but that it also squashes the need for evidence. There is no evidence to support his point. There is also no evidence to support what I'm doing with the immunotherapy. There is though the magic combination of belief and common sense.

Works for me.

6 April 2016 1:34 pm

DONE WITH ZAPPING

We've got a family group text going. The other day, Emma, who was away with friends skiing in Colorado, sent a text saying she'd had a dream about her grandfather Tom, Ed's dad. Felix replied saying he'd also dreamt of Tom. Very odd, as I'd been thinking about him a lot also.

Tom was an intoxicating powerhouse of a man. A medic specialising in treating obesity and diabetes – a pioneer of lap-band surgery – brought up in Germany by a German-Jewish father and English mother. They moved to the UK in 1936, when he was fifteen, swapping his father's last name of Berend for his mother's – Pilkington. He was sent to boarding school without a word of English. I remember asking how on earth he'd coped with that. He'd looked surprised at the question: 'It wasn't a problem – why would it be?' he had answered, in his impeccable London English.

Tom's parents were musicians, and he was an accomplished violinist. He and Pam, Ed's mum, took us to the opera many times.

I, too, grew up in a musical household. Even when I was a hard-partying south-east London teenager, I still got up at 8.30 am on a Sunday, without a word of protest, to sing at St Alfege.

Throughout the course of my radiotherapy, I've listened to jazz, blues, rock, pop, soul, reggae, hip-hop … you name it. But no classical.

So when I was pondering what lucky composer would fill my head for my last day of radiotherapy on Monday, my mind leapt to Tom, to classical music and to his favourite opera.

There was only one contender. I jumped up onto the gurney, pulled that mask onto my face, closed my eyes and kissed goodbye to the zapping as the 'Ride of the Valkyries' blasted my earways.

This is not about *Apocalypse Now* (even if my allegedly educated children think so). It's about me maximising my not inconsiderable strength. Staring TEF down for as long as it takes. And telling it to bugger off to Valhalla on a one-way ticket.

Wagner kept going (and some). Me too. With radiotherapy over, the next act will kick in. The immunotherapy infusions will continue (third one yesterday) and soon I will resume chemo, on a five-day-a-month intensive schedule. The big one to get our heads around is the electrotherapy. If you want to show sympathy and get creative, google Optune, made by Novocure. Somehow I'm going to figure out how to wear this extraordinary contraption. The electrodes have to sit tight on my head and generate heat, making wig-wearing tricky. Which is sad, as the fabulous Carol at NYU Radiology only went and bought me a wig!

5

Skyscraper

We celebrated the end of my radiotherapy and chemo with a weekend in Chicago, courtesy of Ed's sister Karen. We wanted to go somewhere new, beautiful and interesting. We walked all around downtown, eyes focused on the tops of extraordinary buildings at every corner. We went on the water, viewed skyscrapers, marvelled at the variety of architecture, and ate gargantuan meals of deep-pan pizzas, though they don't look anything like pizzas to New Yorkers. We guffawed at comedy clubs, watched movies, were unashamed tourists.

One of the many buildings we toured was the John Hancock Center, which upon completion in 1969 was the tallest building in the world outside New York City.

It has since been renamed, in disappointingly pedestrian fashion, 875 North Michigan Avenue. I was riveted by the story of its construction. Here was a skyscraper that bankrupted its initiator, Jerry Wolman, former owner of the Philadelphia Eagles football team, due to an unexpected flaw in the construction which was only discovered when the building was already twenty stories high. It was eventually taken over by John Hancock Mutual Life.

The building is wrapped in gargantuan black steel girders in the shape of an X. I wallowed in the building's form. The cross-bracing meant it didn't have to rely on internal support structures for strength. The foundations were incredible, each corner column weighing 100 tons. The building gives just five to eight inches of sway in a 60 mph wind. Apparently it can withstand winds of 132 mph. As I stared at the X shapes, I felt my limbs moving to mimic them. It made me think of Leonardo da Vinci's Vitruvian Man, whose outstretched arms create a circle. Circles have no endings; they just go on and on. Maybe, I thought, my life could be the same, going on further than I had hoped.

I thought of my body. How externally I looked fine. It was my insides that might destroy me. I often felt paralysed by the damning statistics of prognosis and the repetitive news that the latest glioblastoma trial had failed. I wanted to absorb the strength exuded by this building. I wanted to plug it into me. I needed to feel stronger, to know that the radiation and chemo hadn't weakened me, but rather had made me tougher, even as my hair fell out. Glioblastoma had marked me with a cross of terminal illness. Like the crosses painted on people's doors during outbreaks of the plague. Cross. I was cross this had happened to me, cross to be crossed by it . . .

My mind raced. Back home, I looked at Ed and the kids and felt calmer. I wasn't on my own. They were strong. They were real. I didn't need concrete or steel or buildings to prop me up. I needed me. They would guide me to my deeper well of untapped strength – and so would my wider community of family and friends that spanned oceans.

Crosses. I knew I had the strength to carry this one.

Words from the poem 'Black Cross' by Joseph Simon Newman have stuck with me.

> 'You don't believe nothin',' said the white
> man's preacher.
> 'Oh yes I do,' said Hezekiah,
> 'I believe that a man should be beholding to
> his neighbor
> Without the reward of Heaven or the fear of
> hell fire.'
> 'Well, there's a lot of good ways for a man to
> be wicked!'
> And they hung Hezekiah as high as a pigeon,
> And the nice folks around said, 'Well, he
> had it comin'
> 'Cause the son-of-a-bitch didn't have no religion!'

6 May 2016 12:27 pm

GOOD FOR NOW

My first MRI since completing radiotherapy and chemotherapy was clean ... YES.

This gives me two months to take a deep breath and relax.

The instant we heard the news, a cold sore popped up on my lip. Next time, I need Valium or something to dampen the anxiety.

But oh the joy. Such a relief. I got so anxious that I developed a twitch, noticeable only to me, on the left side of my upper lip. I feared this was a sign of tumour regrowth, even if on the wrong side of my body (my tumour is in the left side of my brain, meaning any recurrence is likely to show signs on the right side of my body). Funnily enough, the twitch has now switched off. Ha!

Now we look forward to the next wave of treatment. I tell you, I'm so cutting edge. It's exhausting being at the forefront of cancer-treatment fashion. One minute I'm infusing myself with the immunotherapy that's turned President Carter's melanoma around, the next I'm preparing to shave the little hair I have left in order to wear a bunch of electrodes on my head.

For decades we've treated cancer with three weapons: surgery, radiotherapy, chemotherapy. While the world's laboratories have been working away at diving deeper inside our bodies to find cancer cures, 78-year-old Professor Yoram Palti dreamt up electrotherapy while settling into retirement in Israel. No doubt bored with not working, Palti dusted off his ideas from his doctorate days, years old.

'My friends would sometimes ask me: "Why not search for a cure for cancer?" So I did,' he told an Israeli newspaper. Inspired by an equal love of medicine and engineering, he decided to integrate electric fields with living tissue. He set up a lab at his home in 2000 and, sixteen years later, has seen the phase three trial of his therapy for people newly diagnosed with brain cancer, like me, halted because it was so successful. With a new treatment as good as that, everyone on the trial should be able to get it.

At a basic level, how it works is that I get to wear a backpack that feeds electrodes attached to my head. These electrodes carry highly charged particles that create an electric field and attack brain cancer cells. Specifically, they block further division of cancerous cells in the brain. So this is proven to extend the time between diagnosis and recurrence. This we want, as when recurrence happens, it tends to narrow the time window in which to act.

When we quizzed Fabio about the headgear and asked his advice on whether I should wear it, he said that at first the medical community thought this new contraption was bizarre. It was completely out of their comfort zone. It didn't involve any chemicals, or surgery, and for decades chemicals and surgery were all there was. How could sticking a few electric pads on a patient's head have any impact on a tumour as virulent as GBM? Then they saw the data. Now it's thought that it will soon become the norm, alongside surgery, radio and chemo.

Closer to home, what it also means is that I'm going to be bald with great white pads stuck to my head for the next nine months. Plus I'll grow a sort of 2016 Met Ball techno-tail, in the shape of a big electric lead that feeds into an 8lb backpack full of batteries that will help shift those pounds. Definitely designed by engineers rather than fashionistas.

The company is coming round next week to show 'my carer' how to shave my head and fix the pads and 'arrays', something that needs to be done twice weekly. I've requested an evening appointment as something tells me Tess and Emma might be useful here. Not that Ed isn't the most caring partner in the world. But I'm thinking the skills acquired by teenage girls in the hair and makeup department might enable them to demonstrate their particular expertise in a way that complements his support and delivers the best possible care to my poor beleaguered scalp.

The online brain cancer community is charged/buzzing/literally electric (oh dear, bad puns, but I can't resist ... talk about a gift horse) about how to wear this contraption. Did I mention I'll need a special cooling pillow from Bed Bath & Beyond plus fan at night, as it generates heat? Oh, and this also means wigs are ruled out ...

But what really did it for me was when someone online relayed their experience of being accused of being a suicide bomber when on public transit. Imagine a large electric wire leading from a backpack (containing batteries with flashing lights and alarms when things get too hot – like on the NYC subway in summertime) to a head with electric pads on it ... put like that perhaps it's not unreasonable. This provoked an outpouring of similar tales online, with responses that were strangely practical and solution-oriented, unlike mine which was to guffaw in a macabre kind of way.

Some people make cards they hand out to those staring at them, asking for their prayers, not their fears. Or explaining they have brain cancer and this treatment is a GOOD THING. I think I'll wear earplugs.

In between feeling awe at the creative thinking behind this treatment, and relief that its high cost is all covered by our insurance, and dodgy humour at the idea of wearing this gear, I feel ... well. Excited and terrified in equal measure. This is a notable new chapter in the brave, mad, sane, cumbersome and confusing journey I'm choosing.

Back in New York I reflected on what the Windy City had shown me. The Hancock Building had reached for the skies and tried something completely new by putting its strength on the outside. Similarly, the Optune device I was now wearing was all about innovation, taking existing concepts and pushing them further. My time with the Hancock Building made me feel excited, because it showed how its creators had stuck with an incredible project over years and delivered something new and innovative for lasting benefit. Perhaps Optune had the same potential, after ten years of R&D and all sorts of scepticism from doctors towards a treatment that involved no chemicals and required patients to wear a crazy device on their heads. The greater the challenge, the more the excitement. A simple equation that appealed to me.

One day I was strolling in Prospect Park, wearing the headgear. It was starting to get warm. The device generates heat. I wanted to take off the scarf I was wearing to cover the device, but I felt self-conscious. Then I thought, Stuff this, I'm hot, I've just got to get over myself. I tore off my scarf and strolled through the park. I felt proud to be an open bearer of innovation. These two cool dudes, the kind of young men who wouldn't normally allow themselves a glance at a middle-aged woman in Prospect Park, stared at me, then came up and asked what I was wearing on my head. I looked them in the eye, with a smile, and told them that I was wearing a new device for people like me with brain cancer. They looked at me and said, 'Cool!' I thought, they are right about that.

I started to shift my thinking away from looking for other new treatments for my disease, towards using my innate ability to channel my sense of excitement in innovation. I wanted to focus on how to live my life in the best possible way. I felt proud about being an early adopter of Optune. I wanted to be one of the first. To show others, and myself, that I wasn't afraid of taking a gamble.

18 May 2016 5:49 pm

COCKTAIL HOUR

Mine's a margarita. But as with any cocktail, it has to be just so. Combine agave tequila with a small amount of agave nectar. Add freshly squeezed lime, no pips but some pulp. A bit of rough. So, too, the ice. Crushed but not too granular. There is of course only one salt – Maldon – to use. This has to be crunched by hand into smaller pieces before the rim of the glass is rolled in it. For me, it's got to be a good quarter of an inch round the edge. And the glass has to be a classic cocktail glass with a tall stem and wide-rim circumference. Only have one. Sometime after six and before eight.

It's not just the combination of ingredients that has to be spot on. Nor the ratio between them. The magic lies in the mix, because when it's on target each individual ingredient stands out so much better than on its own.

Same for fighting TEF.

I'm now on so many therapies that I have visions of Maureen Lipman in that Eighties ad for BT where she praises her grandson for getting 'an ology'. 'You get an ology and you're a scientist!' I get a therapy and I'm cured! If only it were that simple.

Here's what I've done and am doing, four months in:

- Immunotherapy
- Radiotherapy
- Chemotherapy
- Electrotherapy

Supplemented with aspirin, celecoxib, melatonin, levetiracetam (note to normal people: you can gain subconscious bonus points from consultants if you call meds by their real names, not the brands), calcium, vitamin D, vitamin B, frankincense (oh yeah – and sniffed, what's more). Next week I finalise the additional fifteen-plus supplements I'm considering adding to that list. Then there's the medical marijuana to add into the mix. Oh, and I haven't even talked about the ketogenic diet I'm following. All I need now is Tom Cruise – hang on, I don't think any of us need Tom Cruise any more – or Mr Bond to shake, not stir …

So my University of Life course has narrowed of late, with my growing specialism in oncology, which is a bit tough when I was always hopeless at science. Luckily I took the precaution of marrying into a Medic Mafia. Where they help probe the finer details of a PD-1 checkpoint inhibitor, I default to my historian training.

The most successful patient advocacy movement of the twentieth century has got to be the HIV/AIDS lobby. Through passionate and relentless campaigning, the patients insisted on getting their voices heard. They didn't just craft a case and blast the medical research establishment. They blended a unique campaigning cocktail, while the medics blended a range of antiretroviral medicines. They tipped urns of ashes over the White House lawn. The result eventually turned a disease that was certain to lead to a swift tombstone into a manageable condition.

A decade ago, the buzzword among many

oncologists was 'targeted therapies'. The mapping of genes and greater understanding of a person's genetic makeup would inevitably lead to individual therapies for each unique patient. But it isn't just patients who are unique. Cancer is really an umbrella term for a wide-ranging, highly complex group of diseases, many of which have a tendency to dodge bullets and morph into new horrors.

Fighting with a complex armoury that blocks as many pathways the cancer cells seek to exploit as well as deploying the powerful synergy of the cocktail mix is a route many in the cancer world are now pursuing.

Makes sense to me. But if only they could relate it to fabulous alcohol it might sound a bit more exciting.

In other news . . .

The electrodes are on. The backpack is full. The imaginatively named 'device' is lit. And the batteries come and go. I started Optune, made by Novocure, last Thursday. The company sent a charming chap round to run through the whole malarkey. I couldn't actually understand a word he said, but luckily the website has lots of useful videos.

So the day before he comes round, I wait until everyone's left the house. I creep into the bathroom and tentatively start shaving the little hair I have left. I discover Ed's shaving cream. Who knew guys have it so easy? Off it came. And then, thanks to the

Kardashian gals, I take a selfie. Time to bust out of the support group and seek help, encouragement and energy from the world ... via Facebook. Wowee! I thought the only way to get a compliment out of you lot was to post a pic of the kids. Who knew I was Charlize Theron, or the one from *Ex Machina*?

One of my big fears was how people in the street would stare at me. But what I hadn't clocked was that when they stare, they make sure I don't see them doing it. Which is exactly what I do when I see someone looking a bit different. More importantly, I hadn't anticipated how proud I would feel, having embraced a treatment many are uncertain of, yet which doesn't include any toxicity. When I met Deb and Claire at the Farmers' Market on Saturday, I found myself tearing off the headscarf and asking Deb to film me as I walked around the market. Few starers betrayed themselves. I started wondering about how to draw more attention to my head, rather than less. Why a fake wig when my old hair was so past its sell-by date? Jude – surely Damien could be persuaded to paint some dots on the ceramic dishes pressed to my skull? Let's be proud and confident that despite whatever, wherever and however TEF tries, it Will. Not. Succeed.

Which reminds me. Another one to add to the list:

– Psychotherapy.

Stephen Jay Gould's writings continue to blow my mind. Take this: 'Science is not a heartless pursuit of objective information. It is a creative human activity, its geniuses acting more as artists than as information processors.'

After all that meandering, I think I deserve a very special cocktail.

X

When Felix was little he was given a small plastic electric guitar that played the same simple recorded tune over and over and over. It drove me nuts. One day, just when I was about to explode over this repetitive tune, I looked at him and was overcome by how adorable he looked and how much he adored the toy. I blared out: 'Oh darling! You are my little rock star!' He looked at me and burst into tears. 'I don't want to be your rock star,' he said, 'I want to be your rock triangle.'

Glioblastoma is a highly individual, heterogeneous condition that can be conceived as both cruel and powerful. There is a perversity in being able to enjoy and appreciate the true richness of life, even as I know it is deeply threatened. That is the conundrum of glioblastoma. How are you able to enjoy your life to the maximum? How can you benefit from what you have left? When I think of my life in my pre- and post-glioblastoma era, there are a number of ways in which I can interpret the shift. I am conscious that I have been able to think more clearly. I have been able to exercise my mind more openly than I did before. My post-glioblastoma life has allowed me to be more liberated and ambitious in my thinking than I have ever been.

One of the joys is having more confidence which might sound contradictory. The assumptions I made about my life before I had the condition have been swept aside. That has forced me to think more creatively. And what in the end is life about, other than creativity? I grew up in the Church of England. For eighteen years I went to St Alfege Church every Sunday with my family and sang in the choir. My parents' was a light-touch religion. We didn't sit around and talk about the Bible or any other religious stuff very much. But we did talk about values and what was important in life. We talked about the need to respect other people and see other viewpoints. My father always said, 'Hate is a strong word.' Preparing for my Communion, I learnt about the Holy Trinity, and every Sunday I recited the Lord's Prayer. Church gave me a rhythm and a ritual in my childhood that I found comforting. Nonetheless, my generation eschewed formal religion, and as I grew older that rubbed off on me. None of my siblings or my close friends aspired to religious belief. In fact, the opposite. They believed – and I came to follow them in that belief – that religion was the opium of the masses. We thought it was all a load of nonsense. My parents-in-law were convinced atheists. But now I wish I had spent less time pronouncing ill-informed judgements about religion and more time trying to understand and appreciate the culture and practice of religion around the world.

Where I finally settled, post glioblastoma, was thinking that religion could provide a framework to help navigate life choices. Belief was less important to me than the tools religion provided to shape my life. In that sense, it was empowering. I felt freer than ever to make up my own mind about things, because I knew better than ever that nobody could do it for me. So while religion itself doesn't give me certainty, the framework of the Holy Trinity and religious ritual provides a very useful guide to how I want to live the rest of my life, however long that turns out to be.

Vision, Need, Solution. During my time working on countless campaigns to do with change, ranging from charities like Barnardo's to organisations like the Employers' Forum on Disability or government departments promoting equality in race, gender and disability, I started to identify common themes. One day I was heading off for a meeting with my client at the Department of Health. As I set about my presentation, I found myself drawing a triangle, the three points of which were Vision, Need and Solution. With the campaign we were creating, I wanted to present the vision we had developed behind the campaign, the need we were seeking to address, and how we could bridge the gap between those two points with a solution. Ever since then I've found this triangle a very helpful organising framework. Pretty much any problem you set out to solve requires looking at those three elements. To have a successful campaign you need a compelling vision that will excite people and bring them around to your view. If you want a successful campaign you also require a clear idea of the need you are tackling, and of course it demands a solution. Vision, Need, Solution. These three points can be faced in whichever order. Each element can be addressed at different times and in different ways, but they are most effective when they are brought together.

This had great relevance as I grappled with the diagnosis of glioblastoma. I was told it was a terminal disease. I wanted a vision for how I could live my life with that label hanging over me. The need was the fact that so few treatments have been effective. I wanted a solution predicated on a clear understanding of the need. And I wanted to be active in tackling my cancer. So what was going to be my vision? To trust that if you can get human beings, in this case my doctors, fully energised, they will work hard to bridge the gap between the need and the solution.

8 June 2016 3:36 pm

TO KNOW AND NOT TO KNOW

A wise client of mine, Elizabeth Al-Khalifa, who headed up equality and human rights at the

Department of Health, once told me that the key to surviving at the top of the UK civil service was 'being comfortable with ambiguity'. This strikes me as both true and peculiarly ironic in my current life, given that it came from the government department perhaps most focused on certainties.

You're either healthy or sick. Alive or dead. With cancer or without. The evidence-based trial system will provide irrefutable answers. Objectivity, evidence, data, and outcomes, outcomes, outcomes rule. And yet ... the more I delve into my condition and go through this experience, the more I hear Elizabeth's words ringing in my ears.

I feel fine. I'm on the ketogenic (Atkins) diet. Starving cancer cells by eliminating sugar and carbs and eating only protein and fats. (Bring on the steak and salad.) My energy's up, waistline down, skin clear and eyes shiny. The electronic helmet is a major pain, but a manageable one. The immunotherapy is a breeze, even if the hours and hours of inexplicable waiting each time I go for an infusion is an exercise in patience-stretching.

Okay so I'm more tired, but the bed is welcoming and the AC soothing. And yes I can get glum, hence the acquisition of a huge ball of fluff named Jazzy, a soft-coated wheaten terrier I defy anyone not to adore.

So I feel fine. But am I fine?

Of course I want to know that the treatment I'm having is working. Twelve thousand bucks-worth of nivolumab courses through my veins every month. Turns out we have no way of knowing if it's working without looking at MRIs. And even then the MRI might show a flare that could be anything, from the after-effects of radiation to my immune systems being fired up by the nivolumab. The only indications we have of how I'm doing are things like whether I'm having more headaches, can follow the nurse's finger as she moves her hand (I have to suppress a giggle each time, remembering how my father used to test my sobriety as a teenager back late from the pub in much the same way. Yup, I invariably failed the test). Or my favourite, which provoked an 'oh god' reaction from Ed, was when I was challenged to recite the months of the year backwards. Of course MRIs do tell us a lot, but they're not definitive and don't embrace all the treatments I'm taking.

So I'm living with uncertainty. I know we are all in this club, but the scale and stakes of difference between certainty and ambiguity for me are almost certainly much bigger than they are for you. And I'm finding navigating this terrain tough.

I'm frustrated by the familiar tale of the more I find out, the more I appreciate what I don't know.

Unclear about how I can use my patient-power to accelerate progress against brain cancer. I'm on an uncomfortable see-saw, where some of the time I feel confident and full of clever insights into how if only the medical profession could become truly patient-centred all would be fine, or if only it would apply universal design principles and crack the hardest cancer first (rather than ones that impact on the largest number of people) and so on ... and then the see-saw swings abruptly and I'm met by insurmountables, like the bloody blood-brain barrier, unique in the human body, the brain's most valiant protector that can also prevent new medical treatments from reaching the tumour. Or how my own fixation on all things brain cancer might not be shared in equal measure by everyone.

Sometimes I feel that it's contradictions, not ambiguity, that are driving me most nuts. Rest so I can get over the radiotherapy; exercise so I keep my immune system fit for chemo. Stay away from the online community to stay sane; get support from fellow travellers offering the solidarity of those in a horribly selective club. Add to the cocktail with supplements and therapies – they can't do any harm; keep focused on the main treatments and don't get distracted by things that are unproven and have little effect.

I've got to get to the top of the class. Navigate

the ambiguity and see it as an opportunity to make headway. Here's what I do know for certain:

- We need more resources to crack brain cancer – one of the hardest cancers to treat, but affecting one of the smallest patient groups and therefore too often under the funders' radar.
- We're in a Catch-22 where funders won't fund ideas that have no evidence of potential, but without the funding it's hard to explore potential, let alone secure the evidence.
- There's a wealth of evidence out there from the online patient community that isn't captured or used. Because I can access knowledge of treatments, fellow patients and carers, and track my fitness online, I'm managing my health in ways impossible for previous generations. So there's bounty out there, and I want to figure out how to get at it, so we accelerate progress towards cracking brain cancer.

My doctor quite rightly stresses that anything I do to encourage patients to share experiences has to be easy, simple, practical.

Cancer can be inscrutable, incorrigible and inexplicable, and brain cancer is perhaps the most complex cancer of all. There is a beauty in facing up to the behemoth and challenging its clever, wicked ways by saying the answer to TEF starts by putting human beings and their 360-degree oneness at the centre of the plans of attack, understanding every facet of their experience, and letting mad and meaningful innovation flow.

I love the writings of John Maeda, author of *The Laws of Simplicity*. I can't read this sentence without nodding vigorously: 'We seem to forget that innovation doesn't just come from equations or new kinds of chemicals, it comes from a human place. Innovation in the sciences is always linked in some way, either directly or indirectly, to a human experience.'

And I'm living it.

I came across a list of GBM patients in the US that was curated by the Musella Foundation, a brain tumour group in New York. I pored over the names. There were very few people on it, but each entry was written by the patients themselves and was updated each year. I was fascinated that there were people on the list who had survived a long time – well over ten years in some cases. I wanted to understand who those people were, what they were like, what they were doing.

One person on the list was a woman named Meredith Moore. She was diagnosed with GBM just five weeks after the birth of her first child. She has gone on to become one of the longest survivors, now at about fifteen years. By coincidence we turned out to have a mutual friend called Julie, who put us in touch. I was surprised by how difficult I found it to make that connection. In the early months, I was very tentative about talking to other GBM patients. The problem was not with them but with me. I could talk to friends about the disease, but I found interacting with other people with GBM problematic. It was as if it were a reaffirmation that I had a horrible condition, like putting a label on me. It scared me.

It took me more than a year to summon the courage to contact Meredith. When I finally did, it was fantastic to talk to her. That had a knock-on effect. Once I had made that connection, I found it increasingly liberating to make friends with other survivors.

Meredith is extraordinary. She was fortunate enough to have received a clinical trial, and unlike most people with GBM, it worked for her.

From there, I started going on to message boards such as Team Inspire, an online community of patients, families and friends sponsored by the American Brain Tumor Association, and social media groups, to hear what others were saying. There was one woman who really knew her stuff on GBM. Her husband was a survivor, and she was our resident expert in different aspects of the disease, new treatments, how tumours manifested themselves, what the doctors were looking for, translating immensely complicated science into plain English. There was a different quality to the discussion online with people who were 'civilians'. We could ask whatever questions we wanted without feeling self-conscious or stupid, as you might with a doctor. Sadly her husband died, and she went quiet. There's a lot of that in the online world of GBM. People light up like fireflies, engaging us all with their brilliance, then flicker into darkness.

I got more interested in Facebook groups, appreciating the warmth of the community. People were exceptionally open about what they were going through. Often they would talk about their latest MRI, and the apprehension it induced before the results came through. 'Scanxiety' we call it. They would wish themselves luck and hope to get a good result. Others would respond with personal accounts of how they had got through the worry of their latest scan, calming nerves with soothing words.

Many people talked about their faith. People offered to pray for me, or asked me to pray for them. I found that difficult at first because it made an assumption that I believed in the power of prayer, and all that came with it. Christian belief. But the community I got to know was wide and loving, and I in turn became more accepting of it. What struck me was how non-judgemental people were, religious or otherwise. What we had in common was so much stronger than anything else.

One of the joys of these communities was getting to know people you would normally never come across. People like Brandon, a finance executive from Myrtle Beach, South Carolina, an empathetic, super-fit guy who liked to take as much care as he could of his body. And Prakash in Colorado, who ran the marathon but struggled with limited health insurance; he died in December 2019. A young woman named April made me laugh with her witty comments and rude remarks about our ridiculous disease. She died too. Or a lovely woman from the West Coast named Carrie, who was only in her thirties and had young kids. She was so determined to stay alive. One day I realised she hadn't been on the Facebook groups for a while. She too was gone.

That's the downside to these groups – you lose people all the time. You get to know somebody, you hear their interesting story, you fast-track to a core understanding, so much more intimate than the usual small talk or social exchange. People share how scared they are about what's happening to them, about how their families will cope, about their experiences of symptoms and treatments. They're so open about what they're doing, so hungry to know what others are pursuing, always on the search for new ideas that might help.

And then one day they suddenly go silent. And you are bereft. The conversation stops with no conclusion. That's it.

6

Fear

A woman thought she had a brain tumour, but when the surgeon went inside her head he found a tapeworm all bundled up.

I came across this story and it seemed just too good to be true. This is what happens when you set yourself a number of Google Alerts to make sure you don't miss relevant news, in my case from brain cancer to worms.

Report from WebMD:

> June 10, 2019 – Rachel Palma had been having odd symptoms for months – hallucinations, dropping things, trouble speaking. Her many visits to the emergency room didn't solve things. Finally, a brain scan

> revealed what seemed to be the cause: a marble-sized tumour. In September 2018, doctors at Mount Sinai Hospital in New York City scheduled Rachel for surgery, expecting to find cancer.
>
> 'We did a small dissection of the brain tissue, and what we saw was a very well encapsulated, firm lesion that was ovoid,' Jonathan Rasouli, MD, chief resident of neurosurgery at Mount Sinai, told CNN. 'It looked like a quail egg: Same size, same look, same firmness.' When they sliced it open under a microscope, they found a baby tapeworm.
>
> After living with the idea of malignant brain cancer, a parasite turned out to be a relief for Palma, 42, of Middletown, NY. 'Of course I was grossed out,' she told the *Washington Post*. 'But of course, I was also relieved. It meant that no further treatment was necessary.'

I had a tapeworm once, but it didn't go into my brain and it didn't make me lose weight. I caught the wriggler – or rather, it hooked me – along with a host of other uninvited lodgers, when I was coffee-picking in Nicaragua in 1986. That's when I also caught the campaigning bug.

After university, I came out of Cambridge with a history degree and an excess of self-doubt, I didn't know what to do. One of my classmates joined a graduate trainee scheme at the upmarket fashion company Jaeger. Another went into accountancy. They all seemed to have plans. Confidence.

But I left university feeling completely at sea. What was this world of career plans, graduate traineeships, being organised about careers, knowing one's path?

I knew what I didn't like, but not what I did. I knew I didn't like to sit at the front of the classroom, but I couldn't sit still at the back either. I knew I felt strongly about what I was against: injustice, racism, sexism – discrimination. But I wasn't so sure what I stood for. As for what I was any good at – all that teenage talent seemed to have evaporated. I couldn't think of anything. My acting, my singing, my art – Cambridge had offered opportunities to pursue all of them. But I flunked the choir audition, despite having been picked for English National Opera productions. I stopped drawing, despite loving it and having been given every art supply on the planet by my parents. I dabbled in filmmaking, but never took charge. I didn't go for a single drama audition.

Then I found something that wasn't about me, that didn't require a fancy degree, that played to my instinctive bristling at injustice, and combined a delicious sense of excitement, danger and difference.

Ed suggested I apply to the Nicaragua Solidarity Campaign (NSC), with which he was heavily involved. They were recruiting 'brigadistas' to pick coffee, compensating for the pickers who were doing the work of fighting the Contra, the right-wing anti-government forces being backed at the time by Ronald Reagan. The trip comprised a month picking coffee, living with rural agricultural workers, or campesinos, and two weeks of meetings with Sandinistas, mostly in government positions, to hear what they were doing.

Thirty of us set off in January 1986. We were a motley crew of lefties, from the south and north of the UK, ranging from farmers to academics, though we were notably all white. We called ourselves the 'David Jones brigade', after a coal miner from Wakefield who died during violence at the picket lines in the course of the 1984–5 miners' strike.

I was decked out in Laurence Corner, London's legendary but now sadly closed Army surplus store, with mosquito net, climbing boots, everything ticked off the list. We touched down in Managua in bright blue, humid heat. We were taken straight to a hotel where we were briefed. Then we climbed onto the back of trucks and made our way through the sweat of the city, heading north, climbing slowly, leaving buildings behind. We were smiling, enjoying our minute-by-minute bonding, feeling the liberation that comes from starting again in new surroundings. Judgements of others and self-judgements slid off our shoulders.

As we got closer to the farm in which we had been

placed, the mood calmed. And as we turned into the entrance, it took a more sombre tone. A hush descended as we climbed down and were introduced to Rafael, our manager, and shown our living quarters.

There was a feeling of going back in time: dirt floors, no electricity, animals living under long shelves where adults slept, heads against the walls. Two latrines – stinking holes in the ground – for us all. We were in the middle of the countryside, with an array of gargantuan plants all around. Nature seemed unshackled, spreading wherever it wanted to go. There were pigs and chickens and skinny dogs all around us. Families with numerous children were crammed into appalling living conditions. This was to be our home for the next month, and we were here to help.

We were terribly bad at picking coffee. You have to be able to walk and climb, handle an uncomfortable basket hitched around your middle, learn how to select the best beans, and then pick and pick and pick. We would scramble down at the end of the day and contrast our measly spoils with the overflowing baskets collected by the barefoot kids. We all got the runs and bellyaches and were covered in bites. Neat lines of bugs marched up and down inside our sleeping bags, imprinting themselves on our skin with perfect pink spots.

At first, we and the people on the farm looked at each other across an enormous cultural divide with mutual intrigue, suspicion and self-consciousness. We were strangers, very few of us being able to utter more than a phrase of Spanish. We were intimate in our living quarters and working conditions, far apart in our ability to connect through language, let alone life and experience. But after those first few days, I could sense a pendulum swinging, the mood shifting, an unexpected return of the initial excitement I'd felt for the trip. Wait a minute – was that something like happiness? It was a group mood. We got it together. We started to tip the balance from being well-meaning incompetent helpers to almost-useful compañeros.

There was a moment when I was sitting with a little girl who had befriended me. She just sat by me, staring. She could see her mother and the other women working hard in the fields, just getting through it. The random nature of this girl's fate compared to my own struck home. My niggles and complaints about my time at Cambridge sickened me, as I contrasted my life of privilege with what this girl had. How dare I feel sorry for myself? How dare I not do something at least to explore the manifest unfairness and inequality of this world, so newly, massively exposed to me?

Opening that dam let ideas and insights through, and the foundations of learning that history provides suddenly made sense. What impressed me most about what I witnessed in Nicaragua were the efforts to promote women's rights. The Britain of my youth was inherently sexist. Like every single girl and young woman around me, I had more than one #metoo moment. But my experience was as nothing to the reality of life for Nicaraguan women.

I stayed on in Nicaragua after the programme was over, and Ed came out. We worked together on projects building houses for families displaced by the war. My Spanish improved, and we were able to talk and make friends.

On our pre-brigade get-to-know-you weekend ahead of the trip, we had been asked to write from Nicaragua to our local media in the UK and tell them what we were doing. The media portrayal of the conflict was out of kilter with reality. It was all about Reagan and communism, not about poverty and freedom. I sent letters to Mum, who diligently sent them on to the local newspaper. That was my first attempt at putting my voice out there, and when I realised they were being published I discovered it was possible to make myself heard.

When we finally arrived back in the UK, I volunteered for the Nicaragua Solidarity Campaign, the organisation that had sent me there in the first place. I found myself naturally drawn to the communications side of work. I started compiling a weekly synopsis of media reports, got involved in briefing the next wave of brigadistas on how to work with the media, and started to run those courses.

Three months later a job popped up for press officer

for the British Refugee Council, a government-funded agency designed to help newly arrived asylum seekers and refugees to settle in the UK. They gave me the job plus one week's training on how to be a press officer.

I had spun my way and I felt fantastic. I had a meaningful route to take forward all I had learnt in Nicaragua. I felt proud, and privileged.

3 July 2016 11:33 am

INDEPENDENCE DAY

I've got a war of independence raging inside my head. This is a problem of my own making. For some bizarre reason, despite being a lifelong fan of *Our Bodies, Ourselves*, loving myself, saying goodbye to ciggies and alcohol, eating kale (and a little bit too much of everything else), I'm fighting to be free from my own flesh and blood. Because I made TEF.

And it's even more self-defeating than Brexit. I'm so over people talking about how complex and clever cancer is. What's so smart about suicide? Because that seems to be its objective. Kill the host and, duh, we go too.

Whatever. I doubt we'll ever get an answer to that.

If the first rule of successful military strategy is to

know one's enemy, then I'm challenged. I've had my DNA mapped for mutations – apparently the more the better – and I have a longish list. Not so good is that we haven't yet found ways to use this intelligence to combat TEF(s). Of course this will change, as researchers the world over dig deep into our gene pool.

General Morris (quite like the sound of that, have to say) has a simple strategy underpinned by a clear principle: we fight aggression aggressively, and we hit TEF with as much as we can from the get-go to buy time if and before recurrence, giving all those people in white coats the chance to nail a cure. We take each day as it comes, exercising, eating well, sleeping plenty, and using the healthy grey cells productively. All the while enjoying and appreciating my pretty damn amazing family and friends. And puppy.

Many white coats were on display this week for the President's Cancer Moonshot initiative. Obama announced this during his last State of the Union address, delivered two weeks before my seizure in January this year. Solving cancer is right up there on the list of Big Prizes teasing the world's finest in the twenty-first century. But what I like about this initiative is that it seems open and inclusive, bursting with ideas rather than mired in how impossible it seems to make anything good happen these days. The team running Moonshot are approachable, and keen to plug into the views of all those affected by cancer, not just eggheads.

On Wednesday there were summits all around the country to update people on progress. I went along to the NYC summit. There were two panels of seriously impressive medics. But no patients. Being the shy one, I spoke of course, making my 'patient-power-pitch'.

Power. That's the word I ruminate on every day as I run through my mental checklist: am I doing everything in my power to combat TEF? Am I on top of the latest research? Trials coming up? Questions for my neuro-oncologist? Mobilising my peers to realise our collective power for mutual benefit? Am I thinking clearly, creatively and effectively? Am I using this to my potential as the Natural Born Campaigner I know I am?

Not enough. Must do more. I can't rest but I'm not always sufficiently clear and confident to make the progress I want. I'm sitting on a draft deck, mapping out my proposal. I want to create an app where people like me log what we do so we can measure our progress in relation to personal activity (exercise, diet, brain activity, supplements – all the things I know via the internet we're doing, none of which is logged or analysed by our neuro-oncologists). I want to understand what effect, if any, this has on the enemy.

And in the meantime, provide data – the Holy Grail of medical funding and the clinical trial model – so we get more resources pumped into the fight.

Make me do it. I must do it because I know it's needed, I know it's more than likely to help. And General Morris would.

I had a very good MRI last week. No visible sign of TEF. The cavity left from the surgeon's expert tumour removal has closed yet further. Dr Iwamoto was pleased.

TG

But also, wtf.

I'm almost six months in and so far, so good. Now is the time to use the value of good news to push further forward. Kick TEF while it's down. Check ammunition supplies, new weapons, new strategies.

My poetry partner sent me a poem by Derek Mahon that I keep coming back to. It sums up so beautifully where I want to be. The only difference is I can't just lie here. I want to be able to say the title and to do that I have to up my game in realising it. Perhaps it's apt that I'm contemplating how to do this on July 4th weekend. I have so much support from you, but securing independence from TEF is down to me. Wish me luck.

Everything Is Going To Be Alright
by Derek Mahon

How should I not be glad to contemplate
the clouds clearing beyond the dormer window
and a high tide reflected on the ceiling?
There will be dying, there will be dying,
but there is no need to go into that.
The lines flow from the hand unbidden
and the hidden source is the watchful heart.
The sun rises in spite of everything
and the far cities are beautiful and bright.
I lie here in a riot of sunlight
watching the day break and the clouds flying.
Everything is going to be alright.

Most people I met online swapped notes about what they could do to supplement their treatment. In the absence of a cure, it made sense to look at alternative approaches. People were keen to find out what others were up to in the hope they might copy an idea or two. Above all, people wanted to know there were options out there for them so they wouldn't just have to sit around waiting for the disease to progress.

Through getting to know people online, I became much more resilient at explaining my own situation, both to others and to myself. The more I talked about what was happening to me, the more I explained it, the less scary it felt.

The process of comparing notes with others made me more aware of my own condition. I became more curious about the daily changes in my symptoms. The urge to track what was going on both in my brain and in my body began to grow. If I could capture my symptoms and their ebbs and flows, that seemed to me a way of adding to my understanding – and potentially to that of the doctors.

Doctors don't usually tend to be that focused on the whole person they are treating. That's fine when the treatments they are working on can cure you. But when there's only a 'standard of care' – a depressing lack of hope that leads you inexorably back to the terrible word 'terminal' – then from where I'm sitting that's not enough. We need to feel that there's something for us, something to try, something that can give us that hope. We want to be part of this medical struggle, not just passive patients receiving the standard of care.

Patient. It's always been a horrible word for me, imbued with the idea that doctor knows best. There's a lot I don't like around the language of glioblastoma, starting with 'glioblastoma'. What a horrid word. I hated it because it seemed to obfuscate. 'Neuro-oncologist'. That's another one. Why do doctors have that label attached to their white coats? Why can't they describe themselves as cancer specialists? Why does everything have to be so complicated?

My new friends and I continued to discuss our symptoms, and which alternative treatments we were trying. Sometimes it would be carers or spouses who were engaging in the conversation. There were people from across the country and the political spectrum. Through one of the groups I got to meet Margaret and Glenn, who coincidentally lived just a few blocks away. Glenn had been diagnosed with GBM within a month of me, and Fabio was his doctor.

All these connections started speaking to me. They were telling me that there were so many people in my situation who were desperate to do more, to work together and understand better. There was a vast untapped energy out there, and a power in that, a collective power that could be harnessed. The more I thought about it, the more I realised that within the medical confines of this disease there is a real dearth of knowledge, and the knowledge that does exist is withheld from those who are suffering. We are not let in, and so we are driven to share knowledge among ourselves. The conviction was growing in me – it was time to breach those walls between patient and doctor, to catch all this wasted energy from we the patients, and to find a way of uniting the two.

Darling,

You are liberated because you have nothing to lose. Look after yourself, won't you? Look at your babies, look how precious they are. Remember that however much everybody else thinks that theirs are, yours really are the best.

Jx

17 August 2016 2:22 pm

DEAR FRIENDS

Seven months in and I feel healthier than ever. This presents me with a challenge. How can I deepen and cement the solidarity I have with you, built on the empathy, interest, concern and sympathy you've expressed? How do I do this now that we are past the initial crisis, and into the unknown of when and if I return to that point? How do I entice you with me even while I don't exhibit negative symptoms that you or anyone with a friend trying to evict a TEF would expect to see?

You are probably worried that I'm suffering horrible side effects from the heavy-duty chemo I'm on, five days every month. Like me, you will have known people with cancer seeing their hair fall out, overpowered by nausea, unable to live in any sense normally. Perhaps you've known people paralysed or traumatised by the cancer curveball hurled at them, consuming their emotional state and dictating every aspect of their lives, defining them. You might see me with my electronic headset, generating heat and accompanied by myriad wires, bags, batteries. And you may well wonder how the hell I cope with that in the summer sun. And how unbearable not to eat carbs or sugar ever, let alone zilch after breakfast two days each week.

But I was born happy. Perhaps you saw me this summer in London, or Ireland, or here in New York. If yes, you know I'm looking well. And I explained how good I'm feeling. I've seen so many friends, smiled and kissed and caught up, received compliments and support and love. I return to everyday life with a fully stoked heart.

Help me keep that fire burning. Here's the deal. I will answer any question you have about TEF, how I'm feeling, what treatments I'm doing and why (and why not). You can be as intrusive and personal as you want. Or avoid all mention if you'd rather. I'll answer honestly, even when – and perhaps especially if – I don't have an answer. Because this is my time to show you, and me, what I'm made of.

This summer I've played the whole cast, from mother and wife to daughter, sister, cousin, colleague and friend. Now I'm home and shedding those roles, with the liberation that being an immigrant affords. Of course this also entails acknowledging the buckets of homesickness that come from saying goodbye to those across the pond. But it also affords me the opportunity to recognise my strength. If I can move continents in middle age, build a successful business as a woman the wrong side of fifty, help mould three outstanding emerging adults, and make an AAA list of friends, then wtf does TEF think it's up to?

On my Virgin Atlantic flight back to New York at the end of summer break I watched a beautiful documentary about Nora Ephron, made by her son. Here's a woman who was so open about something so intimate – the breakdown of her marriage to Carl Bernstein – that she wrote a book and film about it. And yet, diagnosed with a rare and devastating form of leukaemia, she kept her illness secret. The consensus from her friends was that Nora chose not to share the news because, in Liz Smith's words: 'She was a control freak'.

It may surprise you to hear me deny I'm a control freak. Challenging, obstreperous, victim of verbal diarrhoea. Fair play. But in this life I'm just as at sea as you. Let's keep holding hands while we defeat the rip tides. I'm doing fine but who knows for how long. I know you're with me. Please stay ... And ask, challenge, advise, share ...

I need you.

X

14 October 2016 7:41 am

I GOT RHYTHM

For me, these last couple of months have seen the drama of the first half of the year replaced with a sort of 'steady as she goes', as I live MRI to MRI. I'm over the initial hiatus, and focused on the day-to-day business of staying healthy, but the fundamental rhythm of my life has changed, and I haven't quite found my new groove yet.

There are some regular(ish) drum strokes. Immunotherapy infusion every two weeks. Bloodwork the same. Brief neuro exam also. Pills morning and night. Chemo five days every month. Electronic helmet changed twice a week. No food after breakfast twice a week.

I've now completed six months of heavy-duty chemo pills five days each month. The side effects of tiredness and nausea, imperceptible at first, now make their presence known, causing me to curl up and sleep for most of last week.

But, well.

It's not that I'm bored by all these treatments (although I can think of better ways of spending several hours than in the waiting room of Columbia's infusion centre each month – hours I will never get back), but I don't know how to construct a meaningful and exciting life around them. And I need to. I need a sense of rhythm, a bit of Buddy Rich in my life. Something that makes me get out of chemo slumber and nausea fug and instead punch the air because I'm doing damn well, considering.

I do what I'm told. I take the pills, I walk the dog, I wait, and wait, and wait, for my infusions. But being good all the time isn't in my nature. I used to think a useful marketing segment would be to divide people by those who, at school, would go to sit at the front of the class, and those who naturally veered to the back.

Well I've spent all year at the front of the class, and I can feel the back row calling to me.

I'm not going to suddenly eat a tub of ice-cream, or skip my bucket of pills. But I am going to go dancing. I'm going to leave my helmet and exhaustion at home and go hit the dance floor. And seek out friends who are so fabulously sensitive about not crowding me but please! I need the friction of friendship to get me outta here.

And I am going to construct a calendar that combines the bare necessities of my myriad treatments with the projects I Am Making Happen. A steady beat with *Whiplash* moments of exhilaration.

I'm living in the moment. The one where patients like me move from being passive recipients of treatments designed to tackle conditions, delivered by saintly doctors, to one revolving around me. Us. The VIPs surfing, riding, fighting – above all, living – with TEFs. What we think about what we can do to beat TEFs is what matters most. I'm not going to spout any more Stephen Jay Gould at you, but I am going to bore the pants off as many of the people treating me as I can. We are all on a quest to beat TEF, and we know the answer lies with me and my comrades – those of us dealt the shit hand.

Let's document how we're doing, what we're doing, and how we're feeling. Let's feed those clever epidemiologists a banquet of data so rich they have to digest carefully. Let's make that data work to get us the funding we need to knock TEF out the park. And meantime, empower everyone with a TEF to know what the choices of treatments and doctors are out there, what the best advice is, and how we can use our very special status to get the action we need.

Better go dance it out.

X

Patient Knows Best

The idea I'd been nurturing was starting to take shape. An app for people like me. Every day I could ask myself, how am I feeling now? I could contribute that information – in the form of data – so that it could be a help both to other patients and to clinicians. 'The doctor knows best.' I want to turn that round to 'The patient (loaded term that it is) knows best.'

A year or so before my seizure, I got to know the chief executive of a small start-up called uMotif. Bruce Hellman works with my friend Jake Arnold-Forster, and we'd met in New York. After the seizure I thought there might be a way we could apply the technology that Bruce and his team had developed to create a more human-centred approach to my disease. Soon I had regular Friday afternoon meetings with Fabio and Bruce. It was all voluntary.

This could be great, I thought. We could help people with GBM take charge of their disease by tracking their progress on the app. This would make them feel more in control of their disease and help doctors see what patients were seeing by sharing the data with them. This was when AI was rearing its head, and more and more health experts were thinking they could get a much clearer idea of patients' symptoms by using AI. My alarm bells went off at this. I'd seen in my work in transportation that technology often promises so much more than it delivers. Our app would allow patients to take control of their disease and decide how they were feeling. We would not be at the mercy of an algorithm.

We took it at a gentle pace, but there was so much

enthusiasm behind the concept. At one point, Fabio suggested that we might not be able to get very many people to use the app – lots of us are not that used to sharing their details on social media, he said. I baulked at this. I had found it increasingly empowering to connect with other patients and their families via Facebook and other social media. What I saw was a massive demand and a huge appetite for this kind of connection. I was inundated by approaches from people desperately keen to share their most intimate stories and learn from others.

The first step to turn the idea into something concrete was to send out a survey. Hundreds of people with GBM responded positively, saying they wanted to record their symptoms, confirming my hunch that there was a big demand. The respondents didn't know me, they weren't friends of mine. They were desperate to let people – their doctors – know what their experiences were like, clearly feeling there wasn't enough out there for them. A group of people came together in the pursuit of a shared goal of tracking symptoms. Daily tracking would provide doctors with valuable information.

We came up with a great tagline, 'Powered by patients', turning glioblastoma from terminal to treatable. Next we needed a name. We wanted to reflect that this was a group effort by patients, and that we were a collective force, and that we had a bank of knowledge from living with the disease. I also liked the idea of making a nod to the feminist book *Our Bodies, Ourselves* which had been a big influence on me in my twenties. OurBrainBank was born.

We quickly secured an independent review board certification and assembled an impressive group of board members. Everyone was there because they believed in the mission. Just a few months later we had more than 100 people regularly using the app and enough funds to bring in support. I never doubted it was a good idea; it had felt like, excuse the pun, a no-brainer.

We got to know more and more patients. Before the launch, we sent another online survey to patients and carers to find out which questions they thought we should be asking. I remember Fabio saying, 'This looks like a great survey, but I really don't think you are going to get anyone to fill it in.' I felt, Oh you are so wrong. Every week I was making a new best friend really keen to build something.

It was getting exciting.

6 November 2016 6:21 pm

FITS AND STARTS

I had a seizure in Prospect Park two weeks ago. And another in the ambulance on the way to hospital.

The medical community talks about 'auras': how

people often sense a change in the air before they have a fit. I was feeling tired anyhow, and had forgotten to take my anti-seizure medication the night before. I'd doubled the dose in the morning to make it up. Then set off to walk across Prospect Park to have brunch with friends.

Still tired (but when am I not?), we started walking back, and it was when we hit the gorgeous boathouse that I began to feel those old tectonic plates shifting again.

And the words ... a disconnect between what I wanted to say and the noises I uttered.

Ed was there and caught me, and our friends Steve and Ria sorted an ambulance. A passing doctor explained the importance of placing me on my side on the ground, ensuring I kept my airways clear.

I came to in the ambulance, immediately outraged at the incompetence of the man trying to save my life. Every two weeks I get Ivy League nurses at Columbia injecting me, so I know a good vein spotter when I see one. This guy hadn't even completed first grade. But seeing that he was trying to save my life, I could have been a little nicer. Ed said later that I had been horrid. He also said I kept trying to take my clothes off. Does unconsciousness expose innate and instinctive bad behaviour? No need to answer.

Home that evening, lying in a hot bath, I could

feel anxiety morphing into terror stealing along my veins. Why did I have this seizure? The cancer must have returned. The clock had shifted. The hourglass flipped. The smiley performed a 180-degree flip, TEF had hit a bracket on my human keyboard of emotions.

My insurance policy of doom and despair kicked in, ahead of my MRI scheduled for the following week. Despite a CT scan done directly after the seizure, which showed no evidence of recurrence, I knew with that dull certainty reserved for dealing with bad news that the Weeble was under threat. I had to manage my expectations, hence the insurance policy. If I assumed the worst, anything better would be much better than better, sort of thing.

In our family kitchen in Greenwich, we had a huge white pin board where we displayed all sorts of pictures and photographs. Somewhere on there was a piece of wood with a quote from Queen Victoria: 'Please understand there is no depression in this house, and we are not interested in possibilities of defeat. They do not exist.'

After the seizure in Prospect Park, I found it hard to keep hold of that determination to win. During the days that followed, TEF licked its lips as it invaded my every moment, both conscious and unconscious. Its tentacles wrapped themselves around all thoughts of work, of home, of family and friends. I felt myself swaying in its power, its grip tightening with every nanosecond I tried to stop thinking about it. It was like a mad, attention-seeking psychopath; ignoring it was not an option. My dietary discipline cracked. My exercise stalled. My concentration diminished. Tiredness and anxiety took over. I longed for my MRI to provide the clarity I needed, to triumph over the emotions and show me a clear way forward.

And then it was ten days later, and the day of my MRI.

8 am in the bowels of Columbia on 168th St. Electronic headgear off. Earrings removed. Wishbone necklace set aside.

I lay down on the gurney, the cushion placed under my knees for comfort. I twiddled the foam earplugs and tried to relax as the headphones were placed over my head.

The instinctive claustrophobia I normally felt failed to make an appearance, so keen was I to know whether the seizures indicated a recurrence or not. CT scans only go so far …

They handed me the panic button. Wasn't *Panic Room* a good name for a movie? Why the same thoughts each time, I ask myself.

Then the mask went over my head, and foam pads were inserted each side to inhibit movement. There's a tiny mirror above me where I can see a bit of my forehead. Why? Note-to-self: ask the technicians why that's there. I never do. But I get a small sense of enjoyment with the familiarity of the question.

Then I'm moved inside a donut. It's not a coffin. It's not even like a coffin. It's designed to help me stay healthy, yes it is, it is, stay breathing, be calm – you had two home births for fuck's sake.

Why is it so goddamn noisy, like road works have invaded my head? Note to self each time: ask the techs. Note to self each time: don't worry, you know you'll forget, and you don't need to know. Just behave and let them do their jobs. They want the best for me. I'm so lucky.

Pause halfway through. Inject me with contrast. Then pummel away again.

OK you're done. They smile inscrutably as they help me off the gurney. What must it be like to know whether the person is doing well or not, and yet not be able to say? What secrets this basement must hold.

And then ... Just a matter of less than half an hour and nine floors up the elevator, along the corridor and into the neuro-oncology department. Dr Iwamoto arrives and delivers the headline:

'It's a good MRI and I'm really pleased with your progress.'

Yes!

X

A diagnosis of a terminal illness is a terrifyingly lonely horror. As a communicator by profession and DNA, I found the journey from being a healthy member of the human race to a deeply sick person with one of the most punishing of all rare diseases upsetting in its labelling of me as apart from the crowd.

We live in an age of unprecedented loneliness. It's an epidemic. I find this so sad. There are so many seemingly intractable problems facing the world. How do we stop the juggernaut of climate change? How do we prevent poverty? These require hugely complex, global and local ideas and programmes that depend on the most mercurial change agent of all, political will. Yet you can end loneliness by making one friend.

'What Not to Say to A Cancer Patient' was a question posed by the *New York Times* a few years ago. Turns out, a lot. The writer was well meaning. So many people found it difficult 'to know' what to say to me. But none I think found it as hard as I found it to talk to myself.

I've fumbled along with the best of us. When my dear friend John Cronk, who married my lifelong friend Kate, produced a fantastic quartet of human beings, had a gazillion ideas for new ventures, and knew his aft from his for'ard – when John's bowel cancer became really bad, I saw him in London. He was painfully thin, beautifully optimistic. I'm so glad I saw him that time because I wanted him to know that he mattered to me.

I feel great regret in having been so distant with my friend Gillian Young, who was at university with me. She was a fascinating, beguiling and magnetic woman who drew the very short straw of breast cancer. We weren't terribly close, but dire illness offers a passport to intimacy. I failed to fill in the application, and she is no longer here for me to say sorry.

When Ed's colleague Georgina Henry's cancer returned, we hesitated to contact her, unsure of what to say. Yet when Ed did write, she replied instantly. I remember a tone of such friendliness, such straightforward vibrancy from her. That taught us both a lesson that we have come to understand with even greater clarity now that we are on the other side of the fence. Don't hold back, don't hesitate. Acknowledge the pain that your friend is experiencing. Show them that you are there for them, that you love them. Listen to them.

But my guiding star was my old boss, Sheila McKechnie. After the British Refugee Council, I joined Shelter, the UK's leading housing and homeless charity, of which Sheila was director. Shelter has always enjoyed a special place in the British consciousness not least because of its birth, coinciding with the broadcast of Ken Loach's groundbreaking film, *Cathy Come Home*, in 1966. Cathy's journey into homelessness exposed the inadequacy of post-war Britain's housing, igniting a nationwide movement to do something about the injustice of it.

Sheila was a force. She had an insatiable appetite. She was provocative, articulate, powerful, savvy. She used to wander into my office and look at me quizzically. 'We haven't had much coverage today, have we?' she would posit. Even if yesterday had seen a feature or a TV interview, it was never enough. I became adept at tactical media. I worked so closely with her I could imitate her speech. So I did. Every time the government announced any statistic remotely to do with our issues, I would craft a soundbite and dictate it to the Press Association, and hey presto it was in. I schmoozed and schmoozed to secure coverage outside of the converted. I spent more than an hour on the phone to the *Sun*, who couldn't bear us or Sheila. An hour of deep and powerful chat resulted in my proudest reported quote yet: 'Jessica Morris says homelessness is NOT fun!'

I left Shelter, and Sheila went on to run the Consumers' Association. But Sheila being the magnetic force that she was, we stayed in touch. She wrote to me one day, out of the blue, to tell me she had breast cancer. It was serious, and she was going to do everything she could, but she wasn't going to let it take over her life. She loved her work and she was going to keep at it.

By that point I was having babies, working from home, and had swapped non-profit campaigning for Fishburn Hedges. I had always been moved by how much Sheila shared about her own career choices, her ambivalence about which direction to take, and how she combined the sobriety and strength necessary to tackle major issues of injustice with a roaring love for her partner Alan and stepdaughter Jackie, and a separate love affair with horse racing, small-scale gambling and ciggies. She was a woman after my own heart.

But when the cancer returned, she didn't write, she called. She knew it would be much harder news for me to hear than the first time round, and perhaps we didn't need paper to get in the way of the news. I went to see her, and smoked a cigarette in solidarity while she watched the racing. She came over and met recently born Emma. She told me that she was aware that most people in her situation would stop work, go and travel, take time to be with friends and family. As much as she loved all these aspects of her life, she was a working woman. A campaigner. And that's what she wanted to continue doing for as long as she could.

The last time I saw her was with her successor at Shelter, Adam Sampson. I'd been hired to do some consultancy for them, working with what was by now pretty much a whole new team. Sheila jumped at the invitation to meet Adam. When the three of us met up, her skin was grey and she'd lost weight, but her mind was as sharp and generous as ever. She was on borrowed time, and she gifted it to the cause that had seen her move homelessness from a charity issue to one of economics. She carried on campaigning right to the end, and her inspiration lives on inside me.

21 December 2016 8:20 pm

YEAR'S END

Last Friday I had my MRI. I was warned I wouldn't get the results until Tuesday this week, so I had prepared myself for the wait. My usual ability to lie in the donut and focus on a James Bond red tunnel, with me coordinating the SAS zapping of TEF suspects, was hard to conjure up. I was so tired – the main side effect I get from ongoing chemo and schlepping up to Columbia New York Presbyterian from Brooklyn – and the gurney so comfy that I almost nodded off. Even with the drilling pounding in my ears.

But Dr Iwamoto isn't any old doctor. He came and found me and gave me the headlines, and showed me the images. The cavity where my tumour was had shrunk yet further. He smiled. I smiled. Ed smiled. This was a bloody good result after a bloody awful year.

As we approach the end of the year – my first with glioblastoma – I've been thinking about the debt of gratitude I owe my parents. From them I've acquired a resilience that I'm now drawing down. Throughout my life, even when I drove them nuts with bad behaviour, or moved to a new continent, they've powered me with constant, unbridled, uninhibited and unconditional love.

So when people tell me how well they think I'm doing, as they often do, and I wonder how that is possible – I'm actually, crazily, happy – I realise it is because I have very firm foundations. I've been loved all my life and I've given love all my life. And I love life. So as we end this tumultuous year, I see 2017 as the year I can inch from the psychological emergency room I've been in since January, to a more public ward. One where I can put to good use the knowledge and experience garnered this year. You'll just have to hang on for the next post to hear more. But I've got some bloody good plans. And they're all powered by love.

As my school motto stated: Amor Vincit Omnia. Sitting here, having not had a single day's illness all year, and still flush from my fab MRI result, I can say – you bet. Love does conquer all.

Thank you for reading. For supporting, for communicating, for giving, for loving.

To you all, from me – a very Merry Christmas and a Happy New Year.

X

If you look at cancer as a whole, funding for research tends to flow to the types that afflict most people, and/or are easiest to treat. It's a form of the classic Utilitarian concept, 'the greatest good for the greatest number'.

There's a snag in this thinking if you are someone, like me, with one of the rarest and most aggressive manifestations of this terrible disease. We're just not that attractive to funders of medical research who, like gamblers in any field, like to place their chips on treatments which are likely to succeed. The safer the bet, the better the odds, the more the money comes. As a result funders aren't interested in tackling GBM because it is so rare and hard to crack. That leads to a dearth of research money to support experimental trials that could lead to scientific breakthroughs, and without those breakthroughs there is no incentive to attract further funding. So it goes.

The more I lived with this condition and the more I thought about the funding conundrum that is holding back research, the more I felt that something had to change. The 'greatest good for the greatest number' approach struck me as a poor way to tackle cancer overall. I used to work with disabled people, and we'd seduce businesses into seeing disability as a business issue by arguing that if, for example, you design your buildings to fit the widest wheelchair, it's the most efficient way to make sure the doorway works for everyone. Apply that model to cancer. Doesn't it make sense to tackle the most complex, most aggressive and rarest type first? Wouldn't that be the quickest and most efficient way to secure better treatments and outcomes for all those with cancer? I saw the OurBrainBank app as a way to widen the doorway for people with all sorts of cancer. Let's crack this monster together.

Let's address this chasm between patients and doctors.

In the basic treatment for GBM, the 'standard of care', patients are essentially kept out of the process of shaping what happens to them. They are presented with their treatment plan as though they have no interest in it. It is handed down from upon high. That would be all very well if the standard of care actually worked. But as we know, bitterly, it does not. It merely fends off the inevitable. By documenting what patients were doing to tackle their tumours looked at in the round, from their perspective, wouldn't we provide doctors with a fuller picture and – critically – access to a mountain of as yet untapped data that could then be analysed to understand what combination of treatments works best?

I was seeing OurBrainBank as a way out of the GBM funding riddle. Build a more robust base of evidence drawn from patients' own experiences, and use that as a way both to give doctors greater insights into their patients' journeys and to leverage the interest and resources of potential funders. In the process, we might be breaking new ground that could benefit all people with cancer. OurBrainBank could be that widest doorway through which all wheelchairs could effortlessly pass.

2 February 2017 5:07 pm

IT'S ALL ABOUT ME

I bet if I took a straw poll, more than 80 per cent of you would have had some sort of psychotherapy at some point. There's typically a moment when you have to spill the beans, so to speak, of what's really going on inside your psyche. To dig deeper, set aside what you think you know about yourself. And in doing so, the therapeutic value of lancing the boil is immediately proven. As you grimace at the check, you also acknowledge that you are different in some perhaps indecipherable way, to some uncertain degree, with indeterminate consequences.

Cancer got inside my head in a way no shrink could. 2016 was a year of shock, regularly fuelled by intensive treatments. I completed six weeks of full-on brain radiotherapy. Nearly a year of chemotherapy. Same of immunotherapy and electrotherapy. I switched my diet to exclude all sugars – cancer's food – bought the best pup ever and got to know every nook and cranny of Prospect Park. I guzzled a handful of supplements with breakfast and dinner daily. I stuck needles (good ones) in all sorts of places. I slept. And slept. We hosted a dizzying array of friends and family, dined off extraordinary feasts delivered by Brooklyn's best.

The flowers, the gifts (I still snuggle under a cashmere delight the wonders of which no words can convey), the cards and the visits kept me up and away from the Danger of Depression.

2016 was dictated by TEF. Everything I did stemmed from it. It took centre stage in my life in a horribly dramatic way.

2017 sees me – the full me, not just the sick bit in the upstairs department – tentatively getting back into the driving seat. I'm looking at me and I am much more than a bunch of sick cells.

First, though, I needed to pack 2016 away. To do so, I wanted to look at the physical location where TEF first made its presence known. I wanted to pay homage to that moment, and to the instinctive and unfettered love and support shown by my friends who were there on a hillside in upstate New York where I collapsed a year ago. They kept me upright as I shook and frothed and rolled my eyes and god knows what else. They gently led me down the mountain top, guided me into a vehicle, using calm and loving tones, keeping my rising alarm at bay.

We returned to Beaverkill Valley Inn with the same friends a couple of weekends ago. With no set plan in place for Saturday morning, we found ourselves intuitively coming together for a hike to The Place where it first happened. There, where I had my initial seizure that set me on the whole GMB journey, we smiled, hugged, chatted, remembered. And replaced a traumatic, unspeakably horrible memory with one of collective friendship. With every step away from the site, I could feel my psyche healing, as if it had been looking for a critical stray piece of the puzzle of repair.

The Beaverkill walk helped seal the end of last year. A great day, topped off with a glass before dinner. As I took my first gulp, my friends morphed in front of my eyes into a flash mob, jettisoning me back to those Eighties student days and my love of dancin'. They burst into song, belting out 'Wake Me Up Before You Go-Go' by Wham! I'm not sure they managed to hit the high notes quite as elegantly as George Michael, but you couldn't fault the energy levels or the overflowing love in the room. Go Wham!

X

Nobody quite fits the titles that are given to their jobs, and it's taken ages for me to understand what my 'talent' is. I've been lucky enough to do many different jobs in many different settings, and that has allowed me to experiment and gradually fine tune my particular talent. But going into PR wasn't without its challenges. In London, I found people's assumptions about PR loaded with negative connotations. One journalist would repeatedly ask me what I did, knowing full well what my job was, swiftly followed by his comment, 'Isn't that just terribly boring?' What he meant was, 'Isn't there something distasteful about corporate life?' At the time I was working at Fishburn Hedges, which he felt was a commercial endeavour to be frowned upon. Rubbish. One of the clients I was working with was the Spastics Society, the pre-eminent disability charity, founded in the nineteenth century, whose name represented a bygone era. The stakes in this work were high. The Spastics Society was one of Britain's most loved charities, with high name recognition. Clearly, what might have sounded reasonable back when the charity was founded was no longer acceptable, so we conducted a rigorous and lengthy search for a new name. After hundreds of candidates, hours of research, input from what seemed like everybody in the entire world, we came down to five names. It was interesting that when we gave people a set of candidate names, their first instinct was to go with those that were catchy and descriptive.

One that was particularly popular was Capability. This had the advantage of including a 'c' and a 'p' that could perhaps echo the 'c' and 'p' in cerebral palsy. But when we did focus research and allowed people to discuss the true meaning of the words we wanted to express, respondents leaned towards names that were suggestive of breadth, positivity and new landscapes. They didn't want something with a narrow definition, but something that conveyed a sense of opportunity. We finally nailed the name – Scope. It was ratified at an Extraordinary General Meeting at the QEII Centre in London by an overwhelming majority. This meeting was one of the most moving events I have ever been to. There were people with cerebral palsy, parents and families, who had spent their entire lives living with the word 'spastic'. It had moved from being a technical term to a term of abuse. When we came to launch the new identity of Scope, the logo was unfurled on a gigantic banner at St Thomas' Hospital, opposite the Houses of Parliament. We had a reception at the House of Commons and the mood was electric. To me, that's an example of effective campaigning.

Now I'm using the skills I learnt along the way and applying them to OurBrainBank, the campaign of my life. A test of a good PR person is someone who can interpret what they think others want to hear when they're explaining their message. I've used this for myself as I try to think of what it is that I need to explain to myself and to others. My message to myself is that I have a choice in how I want to deal with this disease. And my message to others is, let the patient in, and you will unleash untapped energy to drive forward the search for a cure.

9 February 2017 6:03 pm

SCANXIETY

It's that time again. MRI time. The usual antsiness kicked in a few days ahead of my morning appointment. Scanxiety is always the same. It begins with a little irritability that is hard to define, builds with Ed and I becoming more and more tetchy towards each other, and finally erupts in a spirited row at which point we both look at each other and burst out laughing. It's that scanxiety time again! Everyone gets it. It's all over the Facebook groups. The terrible dawning fear that your MRI might reveal the worst, that your tumour is back and doing its thing. That's a constant worry for people with GBM. We know full well that this disease never goes away, no matter how clear our scans appear. It always lingers there in dastardly microscopic tentacles waiting for the moment to leap out once more. At least, on the scanxiety stakes, I am very lucky not to have to wait for the results. I can't imagine what it must be like to wait for days, or even weeks, as GBM patients have to do in other countries or less well-equipped parts of the US. Soon after I emerge from the MRI machine, I'm back up to the ninth floor where neuro-oncology lives, and Dr Iwamoto comes to see us and smiles. Immediately, with just that one smile the scanxiety disappears. He shows us the images. Largely unchanged from the last scan two months ago: the cavity vacated by TEF is tiny, and the lightened area hasn't really shifted, confirming Iwamoto's view that this is scarring left over from the radiotherapy. No sign of the tumour growing. The relief is overwhelming.

I'm to continue with two more chemo cycles, taking me up to a full year. After that the current plan would be to stop chemo altogether on grounds that it will have done all the TEF-destroying work it can do. I'm a little anxious about stopping, as, presumably, it is impacting positively. But there's no evidence it can impact after even six months, let alone a year, so there's no strong case to continue. Equally, the toxicity of chemo means it can create problems in the future. (When the doctor started talking about long-term problems, I felt happy! What a thought: I might have a long term!) And the cumulative effect of the chemo is making my tiredness seriously boring.

I'm also to continue with the immunotherapy drug Opdivo/nivolumab for a further year. I've kicked TEF out, both literally and psychologically. I hope for ever, but certainly for now. I'm good – very good – for now. And that's all any of us can know.

Million Dollar Woman

The other day I did a back-of-the-envelope and calculated that I'm a Million Dollar Woman. My surgery cost something in the region of $130,000. A year of immunotherapy infusions came to $144,000. Electrotherapy – the futuristic headgear – cost $250,000 a year. Halfway to a million and we haven't even added in radiotherapy, chemotherapy, bi-monthly MRIs, and a bunch of supplements.

And yet, I'm still in the grip of a disease that has no cure, that relentlessly pursues its victims to the end. So despite all the cutting-edge and eye-wateringly expensive treatment I'm receiving, courtesy of a good American healthcare plan and a wonderful team of doctors, I'm greedy for more. Which is where OurBrainBank comes in. I'm asking GBM patients to input what they're doing to stay well – from diet to exercise to supplements – and how they're feeling, including symptoms and side effects: language issues, balance problems, tiredness, nausea and so on. All that information will find its way onto the desktops of analysts at Columbia in New York and Dana-Farber in Boston, two of the world's leading neuro-oncology research centres. There, researchers will pore over the data in a hunt for what's working best, what combinations of treatments are most effective, what insights we can gather from the reality of patients' lives so we can improve guidance, connect patients to each other, build a community, enable patients to make better use of their meetings with their doctors, and provide a ready-made pool of candidates to be recruited onto trials. And perhaps most importantly, provide insights and evidence which could unlock the serious big bucks we need to find that elusive cure. Our aim is to turn GBM from terminal to treatable, powered by patients. So that one day you won't have to be a Million Dollar Woman to survive.

15 March 2017 11:06 pm

SURVIVAL ANGST

There's something troubling me. Physically, I'm doing fine. But I don't feel that great psychologically. I think it's because the longer I'm well, the nearer I get to a potential downturn. I've never been given a prognosis, and I understand that median statistics are just that, and in no way a reliable indication of what might happen to me. Which leaves me wondering. With every day I survive, am I truly beating this disease, or am I merely running down the battery of my life until there is nothing left? And sometimes I wonder whether I fear not fearing TEF enough. Am I sufficiently prepared for the worst? Or is that a self-destructive and pointless exercise? If things change, I will have more than five minutes to adjust. As a wise friend told me, instead of feeling that the longer I feel better, the nearer I come to the moment at which I might not, I should feel that the longer I feel better, well, the longer I feel better. How true. A few months after my diagnosis we went to see *The Witch*, a truly dreadful film. As the movie started, my friend Jenn whispered that she was scared. Quick as a flash I responded: 'I'm not afraid of my brain cancer, so how can you be scared of a crap movie?' A flippant remark, but one I delivered without thinking because that was how I thought back then. I was clear headed and confident. Every night, those first few months, when I awoke, I'd look at the chinks of light from my bedroom shutters and feel my belief and self-knowledge that I was going to be okay.

I still feel that. But now I sometimes fear feeling it.

X

Mr Vice President

One day I found myself sitting in a room with around forty people all looking frightfully important. There were medical experts, heads of pharma giants, representatives from cancer NGOs. They were all wearing smart clothes. I was the only one wearing the Optune electronic helmet.

This was the New York launch event in June 2017 of the Biden Cancer Initiative, the philanthropic scheme Joe and

Jill Biden set up after leaving the White House to build on the Cancer Moonshot the then Vice President had run on behalf of President Obama. Biden lost his beloved son Beau to GBM in 2015.

This was an opportunity too good to miss. So I joined the line of suits, hustled a little. Deep breaths, be brave, I told myself. 'Hi Mr Vice President, I'm Jessica and I have what Beau had. I'm so sorry he didn't make it.' That got me a hug from MR JOE! I went on: 'I'm doing fine and involved in setting up OurBrainBank, a whole new approach to moving glioblastoma from terminal to treatable, powered by patients. It so chimes with what you're saying is needed – collaboration, a sense of urgency – I'd love to share our thinking.' That earned me a second hug and then, with his arm around my shoulder, Biden beckoned to Greg Simon, president of the initiative. 'Greg! We gotta hear more about this!'

That was on a Monday. That wasn't a bad start to a week.

28 June 2017 6:08 pm

PASSING THE MEDIAN POINT

I'm fifteen months in, which means I've passed the median point of survival. Not that that tells you all that much – all these facts and statistics bear little relationship to the here and now of my disease.

I'm not daft enough to pass up the chance of grabbing good news. With a cancer as aggressive as mine, you have to seize whatever crumbs of fortune you can. But there's another side to passing the median. And that's the question it inevitably raises: What now? What's the next goal? And how do I get there?

I think the answer to the first point is to readjust the thinking. If I concede anything to this illness, it's that it has stolen the luxury of being able to dream about the future. Long-held fantasies of having a little place to run to in the woods of upstate New York. Or of building a career of real impact that only longevity can provide. Writing that novel. Producing a movie. Singing my song. Making my mark.

There's a sort of liberation that comes with eliminating long-term planning. I've been dwelling on that thought lately. Not being able to look so easily into the future helps to focus aspirations on today. The here and now. Making the best use of the nanosecond.

I get that and, for the most part, live by it.

But how do I answer what my goal should be when I don't know how much past the median I will go? I think I've been struggling with this because at times I'm not sure what I feel. What I'm supposed to feel.

Monday's launch of Biden's cancer initiative certainly

helped. Meeting the man himself even more so. I returned home punching the air with new-found confidence and purpose to get OurBrainBank off the ground. That is no longer a choice or hobby, but a need. As soon as I take a day off from it, I drift. When I'm back on, I feel alive.

Say it loud: We are going to move GBM from terminal to treatable, powered by patients.

The idea at the heart of OurBrainBank is starting to take shape. People like me with GBM will be able to manage our conditions. With the help of the app, every day I will be able to see how I'm doing, comparing it against yesterday and the day before. If I increase my exercise while finding the fatigue impossible, I'll know to take it easier. If I can no longer pass the balance test on the app that assesses coordination abilities, I'll know it's time to check in with my doctor. All of this can be tracked over time, so that with Dr Iwamoto I will be able to fine tune my treatment to my personal needs.

A while back I wrote that having a diagnosis like mine is a licence to be outrageously ambitious. I also wrote that I'm not thinking about yesterday, or tomorrow, but today. Getting into that crowded room at the launch of the Biden Cancer Initiative was more than just a good feeling. It catapulted me back in touch with my own, super-strong compulsions. OurBrainBank is going to be amazing.

We have a slide in the OurBrainBank presentation. It has three statistics on it. Thirteen thousand people are diagnosed with GBM in the US each year. In a country of 330 million people, that means it is very rare. Five per cent of those newly diagnosed patients are alive five years later. That means it is very deadly. Only 5 per cent of applications for research funding into GBM are successful. That means we're failing.

Not just failing people like me. We're failing everybody. Because everyone is affected by cancer. Half of us will experience some form of the disease in our lifetime.

When I think about figures like that 5 per cent, it makes my blood boil. I'm cross about how far away we seem to be from finding a cure for my disease, or even finding the funding that might make finding a cure possible. That's not the only thing I'm cross about. OurBrainBank is taking too long to get off the ground. I'm not clever enough to move it along with the breakneck speed it needs. Why is it taking me so long? I don't want to think about GBM 24/7. And yet I can't avoid it.

Enough with the reasonable patient. Enough with complying with crazy diets and exercise and pill popping and . . . and . . . and . . . Enough with the being grateful for the fabulous treatment I'm getting. Enough with the gosh, how well I'm doing and beating the odds. I want to live a long and healthy life, not write about unacceptable 5 per cents.

I was upstate by the Hudson when my phone buzzed with a news alert. Senator John McCain had been diagnosed with brain cancer.

Nobody had to tell me. I knew, in my bones, it was GBM. So I got out my laptop, and began to write.

July 20, 2017
New York Times opinion section

John McCain's Brain Cancer, and Mine
By Jessica Morris

Millions of Americans will be wondering how Senator John McCain is coping with the news that he has an aggressive form of brain cancer known as glioblastoma. I certainly am: I found out that I had the same type of deadly tumour 18 months ago.

It was in January 2016 that I became one of the 13,000 unlucky Americans who get a diagnosis of glioblastoma every year. I was hiking in upstate New York when I started to feel inexplicably odd.

I wanted to alert my companions that something was wrong, but there was a disconnect between the desire to speak and my ability to do so. Then my eyelids closed and that was that: a full-blown seizure, followed by an ambulance ride off the mountain, and brain surgery two days later that culminated in the same terrible diagnosis that Mr. McCain has just received.

That dreadful word, glioblastoma, probably puts most people off further reflection on the matter. But I have no choice but to think about the tumour that lay inside the left parietal area of my brain every day. And that is a reality I share with the senator from Arizona and thousands of other Americans. In our common fight for survival, a diagnosis is just the beginning.

New glioblastoma patients like Mr. McCain are generally offered the 'standard of care.' This consists of surgery, if surgery is possible, followed by a six-week regime of daily chemotherapy and radiotherapy treatments, pausing for one month and then a further six months of chemotherapy.

The problem with this regime is that it is, as my neuro-oncologist delicately put it, 'suboptimal.' Bluntly, for a vast majority of patients, it doesn't work. Median survival, the point by which half of those with glioblastoma have died, is usually put at 14 months. Only one in 20 people survive five years.

That's because glioblastomas are nasty, dogged entities that do not give up until they have done their worst. Formed from the glue-like supportive tissue inside the brain, the tumour cells reproduce quickly, fed by the brain's large network of blood vessels. If a tumour can be excised, it still leaves behind tiny tentacles that even the finest surgeon can't remove.

This means that surgery can't cure glioblastoma. Neither can the current regime of chemotherapy and radiotherapy, so tumours grow back, each time more aggressive and deadly than before. It doesn't help that we don't know what causes glioblastoma, or how to prevent it.

There are reasons for hope. The advent of immunotherapy treatments, coupled with greater understanding of our genetic profiles, promises a new era of treatment in which our bodies heal themselves. But those of us now in the throes of the disease don't have the luxury of time for the results of trials. For Beau Biden, the son of Vice President Joseph R. Biden Jr., or for Senator Edward M. Kennedy before him – both glioblastoma patients – the vaunted advances in medical science did not come soon enough.

My strategy is to hit this aggressive cancer aggressively. In addition to the standard of care, I take a medication called Opdivo, a treatment known as checkpoint inhibitor immunotherapy. Made by Bristol-Myers Squibb, it is paid for, in my case, through the company's compassionate use program. I also wear the Optune device, which directs tumour-treating electrical fields inside my brain to disrupt the division of cancer cells. A recent study found that the device delays recurrence of tumours and increases the five-year survival rate of those treated to 13 percent from 5 percent.

The hope of such futuristic treatments is that they will give me enough future for the scientists to come through.

For now, I feel fine. I meet with my neuro-oncologist every two months, following an in-depth M.R.I. Thanks to good health insurance and excellent specialists, I am getting the best treatment in the world, which is not the case for a high percentage of the population even in this, the wealthiest country in human history.

Mr. McCain should take comfort in the cutting-edge search for a cure that is underway. He should also take comfort in the great efforts to increase public funding to find such a cure, notably by the Biden Cancer Initiative. But there is one missing element that Mr. McCain will surely want to attend to, now that he has joined our embattled but determined band of glioblastoma patients: the hope that lies in our own hands.

The element often lost amid the high-tech therapy is patient power. It is patients' actions, knowledge and strength that, in tandem with world-class scientists and supportive public servants, will find a way through. By pooling patients' experiences through tools like the smartphone app I'm helping to develop, we can improve the medical advice that other people with glioblastoma are getting, and help to fast-track the recruitment of people to clinical trials.

I imagine most people feel a surge of pity for Sen. McCain. I do, too. But I also feel something more powerful: solidarity. I wouldn't wish membership in this club on anyone, Senator, but now you're a member, you'll find the warmest of welcomes.

My life has been changed profoundly by my glioblastoma. Mr. McCain's life will be, too. But by finding a way to channel the terror of the diagnosis productively, I feel more alive today than ever.

22 October 2017 2:06 pm

MR FRANKL COMES TO THE RESCUE

I stole my mother's Deux Chevaux when I was seventeen, the day I passed my driving test. Not literally, but effectively. I took to driving as I did to smoking: like a duck to water, so to speak. So strong was my love of driving I even forfeited lagers at the Rose & Pose.

My pleasure at being behind the wheel, coupled with decades of driving at English speeds, meant it was just a matter of time before I got in trouble driving in the States.

Ed and I were heading upstate, me at the wheel,

gliding along. Him telling me to slow down as per usual – yada-yada-yada – and me ignoring him, also as per usual.

Just as in the movies, the police car lights up, blasts out, and I pull over. An extremely tall man with a fancy hat and face-hugging sunglasses strolls over. He asks for my ID. The problem was that not only did I have no ID, I had no US driving licence, and no UK one. Nothing.

Uh oh.

My strategy was to up the English accent, and take a long long time pretending to slowly search for a fictional ID, all the way expressing apologies in the way that only English people can.

Eventually he asked me to get back in the car, telling me that he'd let me go, but that I really might want to consider getting some form of ID and a driving licence before my next trip.

I was reminded of this episode when I started reading the phenomenal *Man's Search for Meaning* by Viktor E. Frankl. Frankl was a psychiatrist who survived Auschwitz. His book offers extraordinary insights into why some people survived the genocide.

Early on in the book, he talks about how he was able to forge a relationship with his 'Capo'. These were SS-appointed prisoners who headed up labour squads. They kept their privileged positions by terrorising subordinate prisoners. Frankl was able to get into his Capo's good books by using his personality – particularly his innate empathy – and psychiatric knowledge to advise the Capo over his struggles with his romantic life. He adjusted his manner to appeal to his foe's better instincts. As a result, the Capo kept Frankl close to him, and ensured he had preferential treatment. He valued Frankl's advice, so it was in his interests to keep him alive. This meant Frankl got a myriad of tiny advantages: a morsel more food, a slightly better task – individually not significant, but collectively making a huge difference in his chances of survival.

In sharing these two tales, I am in no way attempting to equate them, of course. Nor am I of the view that surviving a concentration camp – or a serious cancer diagnosis – is down to personality. What I am observing is how my particular personality can be put to best use in front of the challenge I face. Whereas I had thought that the Weeble was incapable of falling over, and that indeed it was in my control, I have found during the last few months the control slipping, and the Weeble failing to upright itself as quickly or as easily as in the months following my diagnosis.

I'm glad to report the wobbling Weeble has regained its balance and stands straight and still.

Mr Frankl has a lot to do with that. As does the

psychiatrist I've started to see – Dr Marina Benaur – who brought the book to my attention.

I have been increasingly anxious. Night-time trips to the bathroom have stretched out, as I have found it hard to get back to sleep, the GBM horror preventing me from relaxing. Facebook GBM groups have enticed me in, only for me to come away often feeling aghast at the tales of carers who have lost loved ones just weeks or months after being diagnosed. Frustration at the complexity of getting OurBrainBank off the ground has been making me feel out of control too.

Maybe it was psychosomatic, or maybe just the cumulative impact of being on chemo and immunotherapy for a year and a half. But I started to itch. And itch. And itch. A corner of one of the arrays in my electronic headgear would come loose. I'd been wearing the contraption for months by now, and though in theory it was helping keep TEF at bay by zapping it with electronic pulses, the device was starting to cause me trouble. Once the corner of an array loosened, an itch equivalent to the bites of a squad of mosquitoes would erupt, proving irresistible to my index finger. I'd sneak in a scratch; enjoy a delicious moment of satisfaction, swiftly followed by pain. And then the itch grew to cover my body. I'd have a shower and find myself using the towel so harshly that my skin went red. Small sores grew into open wounds.

I was referred to Dr Mario Lacouture at Memorial Sloan Kettering, a senior dermatologist who's been seeing a number of Optune users with sore scalps. Novocure, the company that makes the device, has supplied new barrier creams. But my skin became increasingly painful. I would wake up to a body covered in red hives. I found it hard to think about anything other than the itching. It got so bad I couldn't even take the arrays off without moaning.

The upshot is that I'm taking time off the device, using creams and fresh air to heal the wounds. While it feels liberating not to wear the arrays and carry a bunch of wires and a bag around with me, it also worries me. Optune is the only treatment I take, other than the chemotherapy, that's proven to extend life. So I want it back on as soon as my head is healed.

Nevertheless, I feel good. The best medicine of all is a good MRI. Just short of a week ago, I emerged triumphant from Columbia. 'No evidence of disease progression' and that fabulously reassuring, trusted smile from Dr Iwamoto.

But I'm still confused.

I seem to be surrounded by spectrums and contrasts, my mind and mood ricocheting from the substantive to the superficial. Did I really seek to relate my ability to avoid a speeding fine with Mr Frankl's successful avoidance of the gas chamber?

I must be crazy. No need to respond to that.

Here's another spectrum. I began the summer by penning an op-ed for the *NYT*, and ended it by appearing on the *Dr Oz Show*. For my British friends, Dr Oz used to appear on Oprah Winfrey, pitched as a medical expert who could connect with the masses, and who was open to alternative treatments as well as traditional Western medicine. Many are sceptical of him, others support him.

Dr Oz planned a feature about GBM, centred on an interview with Maria Menounos, the TV personality who has been quite public about her recent surgery to remove a benign brain tumour. Maria's mother has GBM, so she asked the producers to invite people with GBM to the taping of the show. The producers wanted to convey a message of hope, and hence I was invited to be in the audience and say something hopeful. This I duly did.

Online, the GBM community of patients and carers reacted to the show across the spectrum. Patients cheered me on for the message of hope. Carers were polite, yet clearly for some of them the portrayal of GBM that emerged was overly positive.

I realised that I had been insensitive to their feelings. From working on OurBrainBank, my mind is concentrated on what patients think, feel, express, want. In my desire to be upbeat, I risked a lack of sensitivity, both for people living with GBM and having a much harder time of it than I am, as well as those close to them. But I do believe that one's attitude to disease is important, even if it simply helps one stay sane(ish).

Maria Menounos quotes Rocky Balboa, as articulated by Sylvester Stallone: 'Life's not about how hard of a hit you can give ... it's about how many you can take, and still keep moving forward.'

I think the words of Mr Frankl go just a little further and deeper: 'It did not really matter what we expected from life, but rather what life expected from us. We needed to stop asking about the meaning of life, and instead to think of ourselves as those who were being questioned by life – daily and hourly. Our answer must consist, not in talk and meditation, but in right action and in right conduct. Life ultimately means taking the responsibility to find the right answer to its problems and to fulfil the tasks which it constantly sets for each individual.'

If GBM is my life challenge, then OurBrainBank is my determined effort to turn challenge into opportunity. From negative to positive. From death to life. To persuade all of you, and all of me, that we can turn this monster disease around and, in so doing, make major impacts on all cancers. It's happening! We have a website, we have some initial funding, and we have a passionate group of brilliant minds.

This is going to fly. And I'm going to stay strong.

X

Eloquently Ordinary

I was listening to a radio show featuring a veteran of the Iraq war who described how he had been on patrol in a Humvee in a unit with his best friend and had decided to get out of the armoured vehicle. He didn't know why he'd decided to do that. They were in a calm area. The Humvee wasn't attacked. He chose – for no clear reason – to step out and walk. His friend stayed inside the vehicle. The Humvee drove off. The driver lost control, no one knows why, and everyone inside was killed. The inexplicable nature of that moment tortured the vet. That split-second decision, made without conscious thought, yet with such massive consequences: he lived, his best friend died.

When I was diagnosed with GBM I decided to do everything possible, and everything impossible, to live.

The veteran who survived couldn't cope with the hand he'd been dealt. He relived the moment from when he and his friend changed from being as one to being separated by death. He found himself caught in a seemingly forever freeze-framed state of PTSD, unable to 'move forward' as people kept telling him to do. Eventually he sought solace in communicating with others. He joined an initiative which brings together vets with country music artists, allowing them to express their emotions. But it was in his meetings with his psychiatrist that he found the insight that got him through. He realised he had a choice. To stick with 'what if?' or to move on to 'what now?'

In my journey, I completed two years of chemotherapy, two years of immunotherapy, and nearly two years of wearing the Optune device. I have been lucky to have the body of a workhorse, able to withstand all these drugs and more. At the same time, I've fed my psyche by focusing on what I can do, rather than what I can't. I can learn about the disease. I can stare down the dire survival statistics. I can face the challenge that no real progress in treatments has been made since 2005. I can turn these realities into challenges that we will and can overcome. So when I look at the scan of my MRI and see no signs that the cancer is back, I feel the vibrancy of life in the here and now. And when I get up in the morning and think about my day, I find GBM doesn't pop up in my mind to depress and vex me as it invariably did a year ago. TEF will never let me consider my life to be ordinary, but at least I'm starting to live in ordinary time.

I sometimes think that if my mother were with me all the time I would feel okay. I recall my first year at university being in floods of tears, convinced I was unable to cope. My mother immediately said it would be absolutely fine if I left college. That was such a relief, and typical of her automatic love for me – she knew what I needed to get back on track. She was with me all the time, just as I crave now. Why do we have to become adults?

2 May 2018 1:29 pm

SEE-SAWING UP AND DOWN

Our house has a cellar. In the cellar is a black metal box. Inside the black metal box are my old diaries.

Inside my old diaries are really boring accounts of what I did on such and such a day, some random year long ago.

The first paragraph invariably started along the lines 'I've got so far behind … I have to catch up … I got the bus to blah blah and changed to another bus to blah blah'. YAWN.

So here I am, catching up with you, dear friends. The last time I wrote was weeks ago …

AGH

Does this signify some terrible bad luck? Have I betrayed you by not keeping you abreast of my life? Oh, the arrogance of the assumption of interest. Sorry. But I want to relay where I'm at, and where

I've been. And during this overdue therapy session, aka writing a blog post, perhaps I'll get some personal enlightenment as to why it's taken me so long.

The new norm of the ordinary seems to be taking root inside my psyche. I had a long conversation yesterday with a woman whose husband has glioblastoma. She's terribly upset that he has this horrible disease, and frets that he doesn't seem to be actively pursuing all the treatments out there.

As we were talking, I felt the same sensation as when I go online and delve into the GBM community.

I feel ordinary. Really, boringly ordinary. My anxiety about where the disease will take me has flipped to anxiety about how far I can take it. How can we engage more people to use the OurBrainBank app? How can we secure more funding? How can I get person X, Y or Z to reply to my emails??

But it feels so good.

I've stopped taking chemotherapy. Two years of seriously heavy toxicity drugs, blasting my system every month for five intense days. Over.

I'm tapering off the immunotherapy – subject to the next MRI or two.

I've stopped waking up in the middle of the night and staring at the window blinds in terror.

If that's a list of things that are ending, it's more than counterbalanced by a list of things I'm making happen.

OurBrainBank is up and running. Hang on, I was only diagnosed a couple of years ago with deadly brain cancer. You're telling me that I've got a cooool nonprofit up and running, with an amazing board, hardly any funding, but with charitable – 501c3 in the US – status, Institutional Research Board (IRB) approval, and more than 200 people with glioblastoma and carers using the OurBrainBank app already?

YES.

This time last year I was scared to book the summer holiday. I worried I might have a recurrence, and our flights might be non-refundable, and what would that do to the tiny pot of $ I will leave them?

This morning, Ed and I talked about maybe hopping down to Costa Rica with the kids for a couple of weeks. I didn't even blink.

It's not that I'm in denial. It's that I've figured out how to really, really live day by day. How to get joy and energy out of progress. How to respect the learning – intellectual, psychological, emotional – that I've absorbed since this extraordinary chapter of my life started.

When I go into the MRI tunnel, I sometimes drift off to Greenwich Park. There's a playground there. It's the see-saws I remember most vividly. They were really long, so you could go quite high and feel as though you were dangling in space, or crash right down to the bottom, invariably screeching and laughing in equal measure.

It's an apt metaphor for what I'm going through.

Year one was bottom of the see-saw; year two wobbling a bit, in every way feeling up and down, often simultaneously.

Now, as I enter year three (oh, the utter joy in typing that number) I feel the see-saw lifting me up. There's a sense of light-headedness as I feel more able to accept how well I'm doing with this bugger of a disease. And more proud, strong, delighted ... at the extraordinary feat we've pulled off, of creating OurBrainBank.

If GBM is about death, destruction, negativity, pain and utter hopelessness, then OurBrainBank is the opposite.

I don't know what lies ahead, but whereas I equated that with fear of hearing that the cancer has come back, I now increasingly see it as revealing the mystery of how we can beat the bugger.

This is no ordinary initiative.

This is about switching out those on the bottom of the see-saw – the patients, stuck with their uncontrollable bodies riddled with diseases they don't know how to treat – while medical deities with acronyms after names, white coats, extraordinary language where words only come with a minimum of three syllables, pronounce on treatments and prognoses.

Flip it. I'm at the top. I'm telling you that the OurBrainBank app is there to serve me, recording how I feel I'm doing, every single day. And what I see from up here is that the digital revolution, the growing awareness that patients can play an active role that helps not just them but science, is inexorably making progress.

My MRI shows 'no evidence of disease'. But we know that MRIs are indicative, not definitive. So, TEF, I've decided that if you're invisible to the MRI, then you're invisible to me too. You'll stay right down there at the bottom of the see-saw because I'm quite happy at the top.

You will try. But I'm so much better than you. I can create, you can only destroy. I can bathe in the intoxication of succeeding in developing something that can help me and oh so many others. You have nothing to live for. You don't even want life. How sad is that. How bad are you.

Stay that way.

X

In March 2019 I stopped all medical treatments for my brain cancer, on the advice of my neuro-oncologist. When Dr Iwamoto broke the news to me that for now he thought my treatment was done, I was profoundly and unexpectedly confused. Emotionally, I found it hard to equate happiness with stopping medical treatments, cumbersome and unpleasant though those treatments often were. I had spent over two years staring down death, using every weapon I could command to counterattack. Yet here I was being advised to lay down my arms, even though the enemy might resurface at any time.

I could understand the reasoning. Two years of chemotherapy is more than a year beyond the standard of care for glioblastoma. The immunotherapy I was on is unproven as a monotherapy for my disease. The hope in this experimental treatment is that it will leave an indelible impression on my immune system – creating a memory that will allow my body to attack the tumour of its own accord. But if that is to work, it will have had that effect already, rendering prolonging the therapy pointless. As for the electrotherapy, the Martian headgear I'd been wearing for months, the allergic reaction in my scalp to the gel on the arrays used to stick the Optune device to my head meant that after a while the sores were too painful to continue wearing it. But here again I was reassured that I had already worn it for longer than the nine months evidenced by research, so it was no real loss.

I've never taken medicine unless absolutely necessary, and my MRIs have – to date – been good. But stopping treatments made me feel as if I was being forced to be a passive bystander to my own disease, waiting for it to regroup and attack me again. One of the reasons GBM is so heinous is that it almost invariably returns, spreading its microscopic tentacles undetectable to the finest MRI and strongest radiation. The overall picture was bewildering. On the one hand, I could understand why the medical advice was to stop treatment – it made logical sense based on solid, albeit incomplete science. On the other hand, stopping treatment for a disease as dastardly and deadly as GBM felt like standing naked in a dark forest knowing you were surrounded by hungry werewolves.

What was I to do? It was beyond me, psychologically. I tried sticking to my regime of the ketogenic diet and intermittent fasting. I tried enjoying wonderful family holidays. I tried channelling my energies into OurBrainBank. I tried seeking a part-time job. Nothing worked.

1 January 2019 8:28 pm

JUST LANDED

It's the first day of a new year and I'm on a Norwegian Airbus on my way home to New York. I've come through a year that saw us bury first my maverick, enticing, deliciously difficult 96-year-old mother-in-law

Pam, swiftly followed by the distressing demise and death of my exceptional father Bill.

I'm flying over the Atlantic for the fifth time in twelve months. The occasions have been profoundly sad. I participated in beautiful, moving ceremonies that sought to express in some small way the contributions of both. I find myself attacked by tears at unintended moments, grief hitting me with no warning. I'm comforted by the logic that points out their longevity. But it doesn't detract from the loss.

My father was a great communicator. He spoke in succinct, memorable phrases. When I was a young child, grappling with the growing realisation that death comes to us all, he would reassure me by saying that he wasn't afraid of death. I can hear his voice telling me this. I can see his face when he was saying it – his expression serious but gentle. His eyes unafraid to meet mine. A special expression for his child. It worked.

As I head back to the States and to a new year I think I'm starting to gain some clarity about the way ahead. It's about exercising the core of why I'm where I'm at: the power I have as a patient living with one of the worst cancers that exists.

What I learnt last year is that I'm not as in control of my emotions as I had thought. When I'm able to rest my psyche, my mind can heal and reset and set me once more on the path of determination.

I'm not afraid of death. I had become afraid of life. Now I realise that the language of terminal illness is a barrier. Everyone dies, so life is, by definition, terminal. When I was told I had a terminal disease, what I heard was that my life could end any minute. When I was told medics were working hard on finding a cure, I heard that there was an aspiration that at some time in the future, we may find a way to stop this disease from causing death.

What I know now is that, because I feel good today, because I have no evidence of disease today, because I'm happy and loved and loving others today, then today I am cured. Today I am alive, well, and embracing whatever hits me in this new year. I can enter 2019 fired with the knowledge that the skill set I have has served me well so far, and that I want and can and will make better use of who I am to help rid the world of glioblastoma. Because the most powerful people in this story are people like me. Impatient patients.

7

Spectrum

I was deliberating with my daughter Emma about how to mark my impending fifty-seventh birthday. It was early summer 2019. Emma looked at me quizzically and pointed out I was about to turn fifty-six, not fifty-seven.

An image of a casino slot machine snuck itself in front of my eyes, proclaiming *You're a winner!* A sensation of the particular joy that comes with the utterly unexpected. I was caught off guard by the force of my glee. A whole extra year of life.

I was in receipt of a windfall. I feel like a prisoner much of the time. Jailed by my disease, subject to its invisible diktats. Most of us mark our personal landmarks with celebrations of life: birthdays, anniversaries, achievements.

I am lucky to have had many, but to have this surprise bonus felt particularly delicious.

It allowed me to set off with all five of us to Ireland, for a much needed and anticipated holiday.

A few weeks later, we arrived at Heathrow, ready to board our flight back to New York.

16 August 2019, 5:06 pm

ORDER! ORDER!

For just over three and a half years, or forty-three months, or something like fifteen MRIs, I've woken to a voice not unlike the Speaker of the House of Commons, John Bercow, saying 'Order! Order! The Noes have it!'

All those MRIs found No Evidence of Disease. Never has No been such a great sound. And its repetition almost led me to believe there really could be some sense of order in my life, despite the disruption of glioblastoma.

But the inexorable logic of the disease has caught up with me, as it does with pretty much everyone with GBM.

The bugger is back.

X

Heathrow Flickers

It happened on a Sunday in August at Terminal 3 in Heathrow. Not the kind of location you'd choose as the place to be delivered bad news, surrounded by strangers and stress. We were returning from London to New York at the end of our summer and were at the gate, about to board, when I sensed a flicker in the corner of my right eye. I immediately leapt for innocent explanations. I was tired. We'd flown from Ireland the day before. It's always stressful heading home after a blissful break by the sea. Maybe I was dehydrated or energy deprived. Please let it be something innocent like that, and not the dreadful news that deep down I knew it was.

I closed my eyes hoping the flicker would go away. It didn't. I allowed the realisation to wash over me, and then I did what I had to do. It's testament to what an extraordinary doctor Fabio Iwamoto is, and after almost four years what a great friend he has become, that he responded to my email, sent from thousands of miles away on a Sunday, within minutes.

He told me to increase my anti-seizure meds immediately, wait for a couple of hours, and if the eye calmed down then get on the next flight. So that's what we did. We took refuge in one of the lounges reserved for travellers in distress – who knew they even existed? – with the curtains drawn tight shrouding the room in darkness. A couple of other people were in the room sitting silently. I wondered what their distress was all about. Were they in the throes of panic that their deadly tumour had come back too?

Less than twenty-four hours later, we were back in New York, I had had another MRI, and Fabio was delivering us the news that I knew he would – the cancer had returned. Within a week of that I was under the knife again, with surgery to remove as much of the newly grown tumour as was possible.

The next couple of months saw me ricochet from doctors' appointments to surgery to expert opinions, and between a bewildering host of emotions. I had known that recurrence was always very likely to happen. GBM is the Terminator of cancers – it never goes away and it never stops trying to kill you. So when my eye started fluttering at Heathrow, it was on one level just confirmation of what I knew would one day come. It was as if a shadow that had been hanging over me for the past almost four years, darkening my mood at times almost imperceptibly but always there, had now broken out into torrential rain. There. You see. I knew it would do that eventually.

Nonetheless, the news that 'recurrence' had happened and that I was back in a fight for my life represented a huge shift for me. I had had more than three years of clean MRIs. Every other month over that period I had seen Fabio's face light up with a smile and heard his reassuring words that there was no sign of disease. That phrase 'no evidence of disease progression' was golden. It was hope. Now everything had changed. I knew that GBM is so aggressive that even if I had excellent surgery – which I did – and if we looked at every other experimental treatment out there, it was just a matter of time. There are very few people for whom the disease never comes back. What happened at Heathrow in August 2019 showed that I was not going to be one of them. There was no going back from that. Although I'd always planned for it, it was unspeakably upsetting.

I remember being swept away by an overwhelming sense of sadness when I was in that Heathrow lounge for distressed souls. When we met Fabio later, he too looked terribly sad. He is not a man of many words, but his face betrayed his feelings, and I was very sad about that in turn. I wondered what it must be like to be Fabio or the other doctors and nurse practitioners, to work with people who are constantly fading away. I thought to myself, well, if this is to be the end of the journey for me it is good to be with people like Fabio who really understand this horror, who live through it all the time.

All those state-of-the-art machines, all those MRIs showing no evidence of the tumour, all those various treatments trying to improve my situation, and still here I was back at square one. I knew that when GBM does come back, it does so very quickly. I knew I was in a place where

I have this horrible disease inside me that is all the time trying to kill me. It's very hard not to take that personally when it's your own body trying to kill you. It's very hard to know how to imagine TEF, to know how to think about it. All you can see on the MRIs is a white mass, a splurge of whiteness on the image, and all I can think is: why is this thing trying to hurt me, why does it hate me so much?

27 September 2019 10:58 am

THE PERFECT CANDIDATE

'The timing is perfect for this, and you are the perfect candidate.'

Back in the day when I was at school, I don't remember learning a particular format for writing an essay, other than 'introduce what you want to say, then say it, then conclude with what you've said'.

Maybe the times have changed, or maybe American education is more different than we thought, but the way our children are taught to write feels more formulaic than our experience.

Or maybe I just didn't pay attention. I don't know how to explain the last few weeks to you. I do know I need to.

Of late, every day I have an urge to write. A need

to record what is happening to me. I'm seeking a modicum of sense and order in the chaos of a most ordinary life of a most ordinary person that has spun so out of control.

Since the flickering in my right eye at Heathrow I've felt constantly on edge, trying to prevent a tailspin. I've had surgery to remove the recurrent cancer, have consulted widely with patients and doctors, and have looked at many options for how best to stay alive weighing risks and benefits as I go.

The surgery went well. The cancer had returned around the edge of the cavity left by the original tumour. Apparently this is usually the case with recurrence. The MRIs showed a spot slightly further away, and too embedded in a sensitive area for the knife. We left the house at 4 am, MRI at 5, then surgery a few hours later. I was left to recuperate in the ICU. I felt fine.

So fine that I was moved to the regular ward in the middle of the night, to make way for someone in a worse state. A few hours later I went for a walk – aided by a lovely nurse – showed I could go up and down stairs, and another MRI, and was then waved goodbye.

From home to brain surgery and back home again within thirty-six hours.

They kept telling me how healthy I am. My body

can bounce back from brain surgery with no problem. Agh, if only I didn't have this TEF …

And no one knows why.

We go to see Fabio to discuss next steps. It's a skinny staircase. He runs through various clinical trial options, none of which sound very promising. I appreciate his honesty, clarity, empathy, and his endorsing our seeking opinions from others.

I now have a wide circle of GBM friends, many of whom have experienced one or more recurrences. Most are in the US, some in the UK.

Ed starts a Google doc of all and everything. We head to Boston to meet with David Reardon, a leading neuro-oncologist who treats some of my friends. Lakshmi Nayak, a neuro-oncologist adviser to OurBrainBank, who Fabio introduced me to, works with him.

Ed and I expect Dr Reardon to confirm that the strongest hope for me lies in the analysis of my tumour. The hope is that something in the genetic makeup of the tumour will match a treatment that is already being used for other forms of cancer.

That's not how the meeting goes.

Dr Reardon says he's looked at my MRIs, and because of the location and size of my tumour – near the surface of the skull and quite small – he thinks I could be a good fit for the polio trial. He goes further:

'The timing is perfect for this and you are the perfect candidate.'

WAIT WAIT WAIT!!

The polio trial is infamous in GBM circles, partly because it's received attention from big media outlets including *60 Minutes*, and partly because of the intrigue provoked by harnessing a disease that causes such immense human suffering and that we have been trying to eradicate from the face of the earth potentially to give hope to people. One of my friends in the UK, Phil Friend, spent much of his childhood in an iron lung because of polio. He went on to become an outstanding campaigner for disability rights. Then I think of Richard Sheppard, one of the founders of Sheppard Robson, the architecture firm where my father spent his career. Dick, as everyone knew him, was a giant, whose enormous shoulders betrayed the superhuman muscles needed to move his huge body and polio-affected legs around on crutches. And then I think of FDR, and the lengths he went to to disguise his disability.

All my associations with polio are negative. Now I'm having to do an about-turn and replace this image with one of a potential lifeline.

Around fifteen years ago, scientists looked at the possibility that viruses could be deployed to attack brain tumours, and realised there were some similarities in the way that the polio virus works and GBM.

They adapted the vaccine, and are now using it in a few human beings – which should soon include me.

Next week, Dr Antonio Chiocca, a neurosurgeon at Boston's Brigham & Women's hospital, will drill a small hole in my skull. The following day, he will insert a catheter straight into the small raisin of cancer, then pump down the adapted polio virus in the hope that it will both attack the tumour in its own right and draw in the much greater firepower of my body's immune system.

And that's it.

The hope is that the vaccine will kill that raisin of horror, while simultaneously acting as a big wake-up call to my immune system to carpet bomb any remaining cancer cells. General Morris at the ready!

I will be checked ten days later, and regularly after that. It's not without risk – I've lost a bit of peripheral vision on my right side from the most recent surgery and could lose more. Plus the area of the irritating raisin is not a mile away from speech. Now I know I have a tendency to ramble, but I'd quite like to hang on to that character flaw.

The benefits, however, are compelling. It could give me more time ... we don't know how much, it's all too new. And as my tumour is being analysed, more options may present themselves.

Against that, I know that when GBM recurs it does so even more aggressively than in its initial phase. Dr

Reardon has emphasised that I have a window to do this now. But that the window may not be open for long.

Let's hear his words again:

'The timing is perfect for this and you are the perfect candidate.'

Better be! Wish me luck and off we go.

X

It was too easy.

Even the best-laid plans etc . . . My perfect candidacy for the polio virus came unstuck. The manufacturers of the repurposed virus started raising objections. They felt my tumour was too small to meet the trial criteria. This, despite some of the best scientists in the world talking 'perfect this', 'perfect that'. The doctors in Boston sounded just as frustrated as I was, but here was a classic example of the problem of trials. The intention of everyone involved is noble: to find a cure. But if you are the patient desperately searching for answers, and the drug company tells you your tumour isn't the right size to fit their criterion, that comes across as terribly cold verging on inhumane. While they were fretting about millimetres of tumour tissue, I was trying to stay alive.

And so one of the most peculiar periods of my life began. I returned home, rather morose, and embarked on waiting for the tumour to grow some more until it met the trial parameters. That was a first. Grow, tumour, grow!

Get big and strong so that you fit the drug company's small print in its trial procedures! Counter-intuition was being taken to a whole other level.

Two weeks later we headed back to Boston for another MRI that revealed the good news. The tumour was bigger. Thank the Lord!

We were all set for the trial to begin when a new spanner was thrown in the works. The slot for the virus infusion that had been allotted to me had been transferred to another GBM patient while I had been waiting for my tumour to grow. And the next slot was weeks away, by which time my tumour, which had already gathered pace, might be dangerously large.

The news was alarming and confusing. I was tempted to be cross with the doctors, suspecting a glitch in their trial planning. But try as I might, I could not find it in me. I wasn't cross so much as terrified. While we had been nurturing the tumour, perversely willing it on, I hadn't been pursuing any other therapies. No radiation, no sending tumour tissue to Germany to create bespoke vaccines, no other chemo or treatments. What I had done was lose precious time, and at this stage of the GBM trajectory, time is critical. Every day of inaction is another day for the tumour to regroup and gain force, readying for the battle ahead. Every moment matters.

In the middle of this surreal hiatus, I received a phone call from Dr Chiocca, who ran me through the options.

If I felt really strongly about going on the polio trial, they could try to find another trial site, though it might be on the other side of the country. Alternatively, they could perhaps talk to the person who'd taken the slot originally marked for me and explain the situation in the hope that the patient would step aside.

I baulked at this. It sounded far too Hobson's – or rather Sophie's – Choice for me. One slot on the polio trial, two patients desperate to take it. That was an impossible situation that I had no desire to get involved in. So I asked Dr Chiocca the critical question that I'd posed early on in my GBM journey: 'What would you do if you were me?' His voice – with its strong Italian lilt despite the many years he had spent in the US – lifted, his speech quickened, and I could sense his excitement.

'I think you should join the herpes trial,' he said. That was unexpected. I'd heard about this new attempt, which was in its early stages, to apply the approach developed with the polio vaccine using a new virus – the one that causes herpes. But I had been told that there were no places on the trial, and that the timing wasn't going to work for me. Swallowing another dose of disappointment, I'd accepted that fact and moved on.

But here was Dr Chiocca getting more and more animated as he described the procedure. It was newer than the polio trial, he said, with just a handful or two of patients who had been given it. The very early signs of how people were doing were good. 'Yes!' he exclaimed, barely able to stay in his seat. 'I invented it and I'd be operating on you and I think this could be great!'

Here was another first. Having been through the trauma of letting my tumour grow, like some Californian orange farmer, only to lose my place in the polio trial, I was now being offered a slot by the inventor of a brand-new treatment that was showing real promise. I would be the first patient on Dr Chiocca's trial to receive the highest dose of the repurposed virus – another major advantage. And I would be in the supremely capable hands of the very scientist who had created this experimental treatment.

How quickly fortunes can turn with this dreadful disease. One minute everything looks bleak. The next you are being propelled into the cutting-edge forefront of medical science, ready to fight the tumour with the best the world has to offer. Things started suddenly to look up.

I felt quite the celebrity in the neurosurgery world waiting to go into the OR for the herpes procedure. And I suppose that's what I was. A GBM celebrity, there in one of the world's medical centres of excellence about to receive a therapy that was entirely groundbreaking, that only twenty or so other people had ever received. I started to experience the downsides of celebrity too. Countless people in blue scrubs came by and poked me, like medical paparazzi. I didn't mind. One particularly nice woman, with an infectious smile, showed us how they planned to deliver the virus into my brain. She pulled out a small 'tower' – her word – that looked like something out of a Lego set. The idea that a bit of a child's toy was going to be central to my operation was a little alarming, given that it would be fitted onto my head very precisely and used to direct the catheter directly down into my brain and into the tumour using a special MRI machine.

I started to feel excited. I had nothing to lose from doing this. There was a chance I might even have a lot to gain. Shortly before they wheeled me away and put me under, I had one last look at my emails. There was a note from the organisers of the first-ever Glioblastoma Drug and Development Conference. I was there on the list of speakers, the only patient represented. The photo of another of the speakers leapt out at me – Dr Antonio Chiocca, who was about to open up my head. I showed him the email. 'That's a first,' he said.

Yet another first. They appeared to be coming thick and fast.

31 October 2019 7:05 am

A REAL SHOT

It's a week after my brain has been infected with the herpes simplex virus. After the procedure, I was hit with a tidal wave of nausea and a splitting headache for a nasty forty-eight hours. Now all is fine, but I feel endlessly tired.

I feel I'm getting quite close to the guys on my Boston medical team. There's Antonio, or Nino, my fellow conference speaker; nurse practitioners Jenn and Dan (or Danny Boy as Chiocca affectionately calls him); and David the neuro-oncologist. I love the way they have a sense of humour. They seem to genuinely like having a chat. Can you imagine spending all your life looking at ghastly charts of horrible diseases, working with people whose conditions just get worse and worse? Devoting your working hours in a place where death is all around you? I wonder how they are able to keep going with so much loss. I admire the ability they have to see life in the raw. Although they are at the top of their professions, they don't make me feel anything other than a human being, and an equal. And it helps that they are able to laugh at my strange British humour. I feel they've already become friends. I thought only Fabio and his colleagues Esther and Hannah at Columbia would be able to do that, but it turns out I've got a stellar band of compañeros with me in New York and now in Boston too.

I feel lucky for that. And I feel lucky that this virus gives me a shot at longevity. A real shot.

10 February 2020 12:37 pm

NO CIRCLES HERE

I'm on floor 10D, room 80, Brigham & Women's Hospital, Boston, MA. Feb 2020, and yes my DOB is still 7/22/1963, and yes I can bend my feet and knees up and down and close my eyes and pretend to hold a pizza in front of my outstretched arms and not wilt.

Different nurses ask me the same questions every few hours, and each time I feel obliged to point out (silently, to myself) that the US being the only place on the planet that insists on month/day/year order puts patients with brain injuries who spent half their lives with a DOB of day/month/year at a disadvantage. It's a small but irritating hurdle we have to jump – as if we didn't have enough already.

I share a room with a succession of very ill people, a curtain separating me from them and their huge families, inevitable 24/7 TV, and on one occasion a woman nearing death, emitting continuous sobs and moans. A doctor came into the room and, standing beside the next bed, delivered a diagnosis to the patient and her daughter in a loud voice that, try as I might, I couldn't avoid hearing. The woman was told she has ALS, the illness of the nervous system that weakens the muscles, and like GBM, has no cure. It was such a heartbreaking moment. I wonder if the woman, or her child, have any idea of the trials that lie ahead for them. I want to scream or weep or do something for them, but just have to lie there on the other side of the curtain, pretending that I heard nothing.

But that's not the only reason I can't sleep in my hospital bed. I have to lie with my head on my left side to avoid the new hole in my skull and the skin graft on the right-hand side. The trouble is that the skin for the graft was taken from my left thigh which is now sore, so how do I lie with my head on the left and my leg on the right? While we're working on this, what about the PICC line which is also now on my over-popular left side?

I so want to sleep but my body has been snatched from me and is being so messed about. It needs my psyche to keep an eye on it all day and night. I cuddle myself metaphorically and soak in the many messages of support and love and sympathy. I'm blown away by the empathy and skills of the nurses and assistants.

X

A few weeks after I was injected with the herpes virus, I found my body starting to fail. Walking became awkward. Lights felt too intense. Dr Reardon, the Boston neuro-oncologist who is treating me, told me he was worried I was doing way too much. My first two MRIs after the herpes intake showed a confused cloud – impossible to identify whether this was a big new tumour or a big immune response provoked by the presence of the herpes virus.

Whatever the cause, my entire right arm decided to gradually stop working. Walking became harder, and my eyes hurt. I had a shot of a drug called Avastin that restored me to working order – it was like magic. I was incredibly relieved. But this wondrous rescue drug also contributed to the thin, over-radiated skin on my scalp falling apart and becoming infected. One morning I woke up to red all over my pillow. I rushed up to Boston and went straight onto the operating table.

I ended up having two operations in one week. First, to remove a golf ball-size area of infected skull. Second, to stretch the skin of my head across to cover the hole left behind and then to graft some more skin from my thigh to make up the difference. I was told that in a few months I would have a plastic plug made with a 3D printer implanted to fill the hole. In the meantime, I had an army of wondrous nurses and doctors teaching me how to inject myself in the arm three times a day, wrap bandages around my battered head, and apply what looked like plastic wrap on the beef carpaccio which my right thigh now resembled.

Then came tantalisingly positive news. The surgeon and

herpes trial-inventor, Dr Chiocca, said that when he was operating on me he could see some of the virus present. So it's still there. I chose to take this as a promising indication that this trial really could work for me. I've been beaten up, but there's a battle going on inside me that gives me hope.

11 February 2020 11.00 pm

CLOSING THE CIRCLE

A couple of nights ago, Ed and I watched Nick Broomfield's documentary, *Marianne & Leonard: Words of Love*. It was a delicious illustration of an era of complicated love, full of the ironies and contradictions that bloomed alongside flower power. Their relationship spanned decades, from intense together-all-the-time passion to separation and distance. When Leonard Cohen heard that Marianne Ihlen was about to die, he wrote to her the most beautiful letter, signing off: 'And you know that I've always loved you for your beauty and your wisdom, but I don't need to say anything more about that because you know all about that. But now, I just want to wish you a very good journey. Goodbye old friend. Endless love, see you down the road.'

He died three months after she did. It was as if their lives had come full circle, reconnecting with the glue of love. They were in step with each other at the beginning and at the end.

As the documentary came to a close, an overriding sense of being out of step with death filled me. I'm very much alive. Because my body can cope with onslaughts. Because Ed and I went all out to find the best treatments for me. Because the minute things go wrong, I call for help and my family, my friends, my GBM community of fellow travellers and these docs and nurses jump on it.

Unlike Marianne and Leonard, my circle is in no way complete. I chose to keep pushing the line of progress upwards, despite bumps and setbacks. Dr Chiocca saw herpes there. I have a chance.

There's so much to do, so much to share, so much progress to make and to enjoy.

I choose to stay strong.

X

Darling,

You and me girl, we gotta just battle on through, we're going at the speed of light. Feels like it. We have to go with the flow, we can't understand it, we just have to go with it, just hold on tight. I love you.

Jx

I guess it was good luck that I was able to get out of hospital just before Covid-19 struck. I came home from Boston after about a month and two surgeries, looking forward to finally seeing my mother Liz in New York – the first time she had come to see me in the city for four years. It had taken a while to arrange her visit, but it was deeply worth it. We delighted in each other's company. She noted every change in the house since she'd last visited, admired the new deck, loved the emerging garden, revelling in the new shoots of spring, and fell predictably in love with Jazzy. And then the world changed.

We acted quickly, conscious that Covid was unlikely to be a short episode. We decided that we needed to get Mum home as soon as possible. I felt terribly upset that she was leaving. Despite having only a few days together, seeing her happy and enjoying new surroundings had bolstered the family. It was a wrench taking her after just one week back to JFK for an unscheduled early return to the UK.

Further drama followed to the north. Felix and Emma jumped in a hire car and drove to pick up Tess in Montreal where she was at McGill University, not knowing how long we might be stranded as a family. Then all five of us hunkered down in Brooklyn. There were echoes in this shockingly fast turn of events of the horrible speed with which my life changed from one of health to one of living with glioblastoma. Life changed for me in an instant then, and now it had changed again, except this time it transformed the lives of everyone. We had all contracted the sickness of lockdown together. There are other very poignant similarities for me between my illness and Covid. I had been forced to deal with uncertainty; now everyone around the globe knows how it feels. Living with glioblastoma has forced me to appreciate life more, be more conscious of it. Now everyone is being forced to question what it is all about, what they as individuals can do, both for themselves and as a community. I don't understand how people can go to Florida beaches and pretend this doesn't involve them. I don't understand why we think we are isolated individuals. We are humans, connected through thoughts, conscious and unconscious. We may all be living at a social distance from each other, but Covid has shown us now more than ever that living as separate individuals is not a choice – we have so much more to gain working together.

27 April 2020 7:46 am

GETTING HARDER

This week Ed and I ventured into the outside world for my next regular MRI. The doctors had suggested I switch hospital visits from Boston to New York to make negotiating Covid easier. We hired a Zipcar, Ed sanitised it religiously, I wore my extraordinary helmet that the doctors insist I wear in case I fall on to the hole in my skull. We had medical masks. Columbia felt like a ghost town. The hospital was weirdly empty and quiet. Scenes from TV news of people running around with Covid patients near to death contrasted hugely with the non-acute settings. The MRI department was quiet, the infusion department quiet. I felt momentarily happy to see how much care patients are taking to keep socially distant. We might be seriously ill, but we still want to stay alive for as long as possible.

I knocked my glasses onto the floor. The nurse immediately cleaned them with disinfectant. She still thought my life mattered, so I had better think that too. I've got to stay strong.

At the end of the MRI I got a disk of the images and sent it up to Boston. Two days later I received the results. Headline news: there is a small amount of progress. And that is a good headline. The MRI shows there is some herpes, and a lot of inflammation. The docs don't know precisely what this constitutes, but they did say the area of abnormal activity showing up on the scan was shrinking a little bit. They also said that there was a hint that the abnormal activity might reflect more inflammation from the herpes treatment than activity from the tumour itself.

While this is some progress, I'm finding it difficult to manage the symptoms of the disease. I have suffered some permanent damage to my peripheral vision, and it's incredibly irritating. I'm typing this blog to you through a combination of Ed and my nephew Milo taking dictation, and me desperately trying to master Google's audio-typing function. I expect this is a matter of time and will get easier. Just as I'm getting into my stride with these blogs, it feels like the chance to communicate through writing has been snatched away from me. That's how I feel about TEF – it's stealing things from me. My sight, my hope, my life ...

I've got to get into a better frame of mind. I think the answer is drugs. I've asked Dr Benaur, the psychiatrist who has been such help to me but whom I haven't seen for several months, for a consultation. I think I need more Prozac, which I haven't had for ages, but which helped me previously. I'm irritable, and I hate hearing myself like that, but I can't seem to help it. I just want to tell myself to Shut the F Up.

The mood swings I was struggling with weren't alleviated by what I was hearing from ostensibly authoritative figures like Henry Marsh, whose book I came across at around this time. Marsh is one of the world's most notable neurosurgeons, feted wherever he goes. He has clearly helped hundreds, if not thousands, of people with his technical expertise in the operating theatre. I had been enjoying his book *Do No Harm*, in which he comes across as a congenial, highly intelligent man who is keen to help people.

But then page 57 stopped me in my tracks. It said:

> Sometimes I discuss with my neurosurgical colleagues what we would do if we – as neurosurgeons and without any illusions about how little treatment achieves – were diagnosed with a malignant brain tumour. I usually say that I hope that I would commit suicide but you never know for certain what you will decide until it happens.

How could he have written this? I can understand his writing this line if he were me. I can't understand writing it if I were him. The lack of empathy demonstrated here felt cruel. I was shocked, stunned, when I read it. I went over and over the passage, trying to convince myself that I must have misread it, that it was my mistake. Here was a man who is a legend in his field, who doctors around the world look up to for his deep insights into the medicine of the brain. Here was a person who for people like me represented hope – he was our path to survival. I'd even heard him on *Desert Island Discs* on the radio, sharing his life story and his most intimate musical moments.

He sounded profoundly sympathetic, a professional who cared about his patients and the help he could give them. But here, in just two sentences, he had destroyed all that, torn it up. In those two sentences he had stripped me of my personhood. He had deprived me of any ability to play a role in my own mortality. I had become just an object to him, a thing with GBM, who if I had the guts would kill myself.

I imagined what it would be like telling Henry Marsh to his face what I think of page 57. But in the end I concluded it wouldn't be worth my time, and time continues to be my most precious currency. I needed time to understand what was happening to me. I needed time to figure out how to make the best use of the time I had left. I needed time to work on OurBrainBank, which through our social media contacts with GBM patients and families around the world was really taking off.

So instead of wasting time on Marsh, I transferred my focus to Jules Taylor. She expressed her feelings on Facebook to the community of people like us with glioblastoma. Her single post made more of a positive impression on me than Marsh's entire book.

She said: 'If we can put a man on the moon, have at least five erectile dysfunction drugs, turn an egg into a full-grown chicken in three days, and for heaven's sake have our elections rigged by Russians, then don't fucking tell me we can't find a cure for cancer!'

That was my kind of thinking.

A strange thing has happened to me as I go through what I am having to come to terms with as the later stages of my illness. Having been relatively alone in this journey for the past four years, wrestling with a very rare disease, I now find that the rest of the world has joined me.

We are all fighting for our survival now. At times it has felt as though I'm the only person on the planet who is so obsessed with staying alive. Now, everybody is obsessed, just like me. Though coronavirus has laid bare the terrible injustices of the modern world – not least in America with the hideous inequalities of race and income being directly reflected in death rates from Covid-19 – it has also been a great leveller, bringing us all together in a united desire to live.

So there has been a lot to be thankful for at this time of great suffering. The virus has also thrown my family together in a way that I couldn't have imagined, bringing all five of us under the same roof for months on end at exactly the point when I needed the support most. I'm grateful for that too.

At times I can't help reflecting on the disparity in all this. More than $9bn has been pumped by the US government into finding a coronavirus vaccine. As it should be. Meanwhile, barely any new treatments for GBM are being developed at trial because of the dearth of funds. I get it. Glioblastoma is a rare disease and there aren't enough of us to get politicians and money people excited. Does that mean my life is worthless?

When I have these thoughts, I try and push the anger that wells up within me away and turn it into determination. Where there is a will, there is a way. We've seen that with coronavirus and the race for a vaccine. So we just have to find a way of generating the will. We have to persuade people that finding a cure to GBM matters, not just for people like me but for all of us, for all our futures. If we care enough, together, we can accomplish what we thought was impossible.

8

An Expression of Sadness

Fabio had a patient who, when told he had glioblastoma, didn't react in the way most people do. He didn't say: 'Why me?' Instead, he responded: 'Why not me?'

Before my cancer returned, I held out hope that I could be one of the lucky few whose glioblastoma seemed to disappear for no clear reason. Once it had come back, I could no longer think like that, and inevitably I found my belief in my own ability to survive fading. When glioblastoma returns, it tends to make its presence known very rapidly.

I had been quite taken aback by Fabio's expression when Ed and I went to see him at Columbia University hospital after the MRI that confirmed the recurrence. I was in urgent fighting mode wanting to hear what the MRI showed, already knowing that the flicker meant the worst, and unable to accept that there might be anything other than some choices still ahead. But Fabio's face seemed for the first time to be imbued with great sadness. Ed and I came away saddened by his sadness. I didn't want sadness, I wanted action. I didn't want confirmation of the worst, I wanted options for how to tackle it. That frustration passed very quickly. But the moment when my leading doctor dropped his guard and allowed me to witness his sorrow for my condition was very significant. In time, I was able to appreciate it for what it was: a sign of his true solidarity with me as his patient and friend. My life matters to him.

In the course of my time with Fabio, he had treated me with cutting-edge immunotherapy, extended my chemotherapy, and introduced me to the Martian tumour-zapping headgear, Novocure. Through it all, I realised what an extraordinary journey I have been on with him, always looking for new options – new hope – yet always focused on my specific circumstances. I wonder often what it must be like to be Fabio and other doctors like him, so determined to help people, yet so often having to face the disappointment of losing them. To have to watch your patients die over and over. How hard that must be.

I went on to have four brain surgeries in as many months.

Those procedures, conducted in Boston at Brigham & Women's Hospital where I had been given the groundbreaking herpes virus, included two operations that were 'awake craniotomies'. Such a polite way of describing having a knife stuck into your brain while you are sitting there fully compos mentis. I say that, though I can't remember a single thing about either procedure. Much to my surprise, one of the surgeons came to see me in my hospital bed a couple of days after the second awake craniotomy and presented me with a university scarf from my old alma mater. That's lovely, I told him, but why are you giving me a Cambridge University scarf? He explained that he had spent a year at Cambridge himself as part of his surgical training. Then he told me that during several hours of surgery, I'd wittered on incessantly about my childhood in Greenwich and my college years. He was so moved by my description that he decided to give me his prized possession of the scarf. I have no idea what I said, but it must have been impressive.

It also did the trick. By talking while they dug around in my skull, I allowed Dr Chiocca and his colleagues to press on further down into my brain than they might otherwise have done because they could tell when they were reaching the sensitive areas that control speech. As soon as I began to speak gobbledygook, they knew to stop. After the second awake craniotomy, Dr Chiocca told me he'd got 99 per cent of all the tumour he could see out of me.

Such promising news, only to have our hopes quickly dashed. With each new surgery, and despite removing large portions of the physical tumour, it became clearer that the herpes, which had offered such hope, had not worked for me. As Dr Chiocca explained it, my tumour had managed to escape the grasp of the virus and had begun extending its tentacles to parts of my brain that the injected virus could not reach. Though there were indications that it had been actively attacking the tumour, and promoting an immune response from my body, it was not sufficient to prevent the cancer growing again.

That is the cold, medical explanation in any case. On a personal level, it meant the worst. It was that moment that had been looming over me from day one with the seizure in the hills of upstate New York. Over the ensuing four years, I had tried so much, experimented with the latest that science had to offer, been resolute in staying positive and determined, yet in the end it hadn't worked. The tumour got to win. My options were running out.

The crunch moment came in Boston. We had been called back up to the city from New York for another MRI, about three weeks after the latest awake craniotomy had removed all that tumour. I had ominous feelings about it for days before we went – the normal 'scanxiety' ramped up to almost unbearable levels. The instant Dr Chiocca entered the consulting room, it was obvious.

His usual buoyant mood was missing, his smile no longer encouraging but empathetic.

He told me that in the space of just three short weeks all that tumour he had got out had grown straight back, as though it were completely unfazed by anything flung at it. It wasn't time to give up hope, Dr Chiocca told me. But the road was getting harder. At this stage, GBM becomes increasingly difficult to fight because it keeps changing its form, like a character out of a horror film, evading all known treatments. He proposed hitting it with another round of standard-of-care therapies – radiation and chemotherapy that had worked for me back in the beginning. But there was an unmistakable demeanour to him, and I had to ask.

'And if those treatments don't work? How long have I got?'

He paused for quite a while, his face not hiding the painful thinking he was doing.

'Worst case scenario?' he said.

'Worst case scenario,' I replied.

'Three to six months.'

Ed and I often indulge in speculation about our retirement. A little house somewhere upstate, a small garden plot for vegetables, space to walk the dog, read our favourite books . . . I could go on. That's another cruelty of GBM. Glioblastoma hits, for the most part, in middle age, just when we are getting to a point where we can replace the ambition of youth with a growing realisation that the half-empty glass might not be so bad. This is when we start to imagine what life could be like, only to have that fantasy ripped from us by this disease.

The flip side of that is that being so ill has sharpened my senses. I can see how I have grown in confidence even while my ability to control my life has diminished. I have met so many people living with this disease, and their partners who are deeply involved, and it has been a humbling experience. We are stripped of our assumptions about health and about life. And while that leads to bitter disappointment, there is a liberation to knowing that all bets are off.

My children have gone from teenagers to young adults during the nearly five years I've been living with this disease. All are leading happy lives. They are full of ideas. Ed has become an even better partner than he was before. This family, that I am so lucky to be part of, has demonstrated collective spirit to go beyond adversity. Happiness has always been my north star and that's where it remains.

I might still be devoted to happiness. But that doesn't mean I am delusional. With the failure of the herpes treatment – that one big shot I had at longevity after the tumour returned – it was clear that the odds had moved against me. As I write, I am doing another two-week course of radiation and chemotherapy – back where I began with the treatment that forms the 'standard of care'. And after that? Then what?

I can hardly bear to write the words I am about to. I am going to die. I don't want to write them because I don't want to accept them. I'm happy, and my family is happy, and I don't see why we should have to have that jeopardised. I imagine what the end of my life will be. Not surprisingly, I find it terribly hard. On one level, we all face this same ending. But on another level, it's completely new to me. There is an organisation called End Well. I shy away from it. I'm scared. I have no problem talking about my disease and little problem talking about my life ending early because of it. But I shy away from it because it feels terrifying to me. My whole life has been full of options, but suddenly there aren't going to be any.

The worst part of it is the feeling of loneliness. For these past almost five years I have been on a journey with my loved ones and friends around me. It's as though we have been through the wars together, holding tight to one another. Now, with my time running short, I am being prised away from those I love and set on another path where they cannot follow me. I am on my own.

I'm trying to work out how to deal with death, and with the knowledge that hope is slowly leaving me. I've travelled all this way, negotiated so many hurdles, and now I have one last thing to do, and when that is done that's it.

I'm full of questions: when and how, what will it be like, will it be a horrible death, will it be very uncomfortable? How will the kids cope seeing their mother in such distress? Will I be in awful pain? Will it drag on so long that I will beg for an exit? I'm not quite ready to confront these questions yet, but I can sense that point is getting closer. The idea of an absolute end. How unthinkably sad that is for me and those around me.

When we launched the OurBrainBank app in the US in March 2018, we were announcing something new, setting something in motion, making news. This is my stock in trade. I love launches because they inject energy, they pull people together and they generate excitement. Something new is born.

One of the challenges of working with other people is that you have to compromise and find a way to coexist. I think my proudest achievement with OurBrainBank is that the community of people most closely associated with the organisation are just a wonderful group. We respect each other, listen to each other, share ideas, and love what we do. And most of the time, we have a great time. What is life about? Enjoyment, but also achievement, and I think that's just what we have done.

I hope I have been able to demonstrate how joining ambition with pragmatism is invariably a great combination.

I hope I am able to show that you don't need huge

amounts of money to make an impact when you have great ideas.

I hope I've demonstrated that if we can treat cancer as a disease that affects every one of us, then we will have a greater sense of community and commitment to defeat it. I hope I've been able to show that while my brain is under attack, enough of it is still there to make its mark.

I've lived through two periods of my life: before tumour, BT, and after tumour, AT. Most people with glioblastoma develop the disease at a time when they have already formed a reasonable sense of their capabilities, of the arc of their lives. But I have always felt a gnawing sense of inadequacy. I've always felt that I – like everyone on the planet – was born with immense potential. As the hourglass of my life tips from being largely full to largely empty, the sand trickling inexorably away, I've been consumed by an urgency to fulfil my ambition. OurBrainBank has been the culmination of that, and so much more.

For me, it has been a statement to the world that I, and all my fellow travellers living with GBM, are not 'standard of care'. We are unique souls living on the edge. When we can rise above the terror, we draw on untapped sources of strength, in ourselves and those around us. Like explorers, we discover reservoirs that contain vast riches of power and insights.

I was given a gift of a life. Confronting the unexpected

has made me sharpen my game. There is so much more I want to do and can do. Most of us feel the same about each other, I think. Life is a choice and mine is tested – the more it tests me, the more value it has provided.

It's a bit like the sourdough that Ed bakes throughout the pandemic. The bread rises, as if by magic. I too will continue to rise.

Epilogue

22 July 2037

When you lie on the beach and look at the sea, the horizon seems higher than your feet, which is odd because we know the world is round and slopes away from us, downwards, until it comes back to where we began.

Life on the island off the south-west coast of Ireland, where I've spent time every year since I was two, is like floating on the ocean. My family is setting off for a walk in weather that the Irish call 'soft'. There are tiny spots of water in the grey air that floats around you, keeping you guessing whether they'll develop into proper raindrops or simply vanish. A pale English translation might be 'drizzle'. I don't think Americans have the need for a word to describe this, living as they do in a more brutal climate of extremes.

Ed and Tess chat about the subject, a familiar angle on the never-ending, daily addictive hit of a discussion of the weather. The sun starts to peek out and soon people are taking off their coats to use as makeshift baskets for the wild mushrooms they find in the tall grass. They set their faces against the westerly breeze as the sun sits overhead, having beaten the clouds to put its stamp on the day. It's a beaut.

Clambering over old stone walls, taking care not to fall into the ravines that run along the coast, they reach their destination. It is an oxymoron of nature: a calm paddling pool of water and beach enclosed by rocks, the Atlantic surging at the edges. Minuscule stones hide the treasure of cowrie shells – tiny ridged shells, smaller than the nail on my little toe, rolled into conchiglie pasta, snuggled into a sauce of pebbles. They compete to find the most, the enticement being the ratio of shells to stones and sand; there are just enough cowries to encourage you to have hope, but not so many that it's easy to find them. The winner has to work for it.

It's the grandchildren who enjoy the annual hunt most. The adults' reward is to see their offspring, and their offspring's offspring, repeat the tradition from years back. They look out at a horizon interrupted by the last islands the Irish saw when they set off, by boat, to the east coast of America, in their hordes, where they started life over.

Felix and his gang get out the Guinness, Cidona and water. It's after lunch, so no need for a big picnic. Always a chance for a bar of Dairy Milk. Emma turns the children's squabble over the goodies into a lesson in calm negotiation. Instead of 'I want the Tiffin,' it becomes, 'I'll trade you your bar of Tiffin for mine of Fruit and Nut.' It's a ritual rumble, not a real fight.

All the parents and grandparents join in, munching chocolate, chatting, singing and hunting, hunting for those cowries . . . The winner's prize is to bask in the self-satisfaction of having beaten all the others.

'Why is nature called "Mother Nature"?' queries Tess. 'It's a mystery to me why we call nature "mother" when it's an unpredictable, uncontrollable, life-defining force. People still assume women are more passive and receptive to orders given by men. We know that's not true, so why don't we rename it "person" nature?' And so the group gets stuck into a debate about gender identities and language. The oldest walk calmly behind them as they all head home, impressed by the growing sophistication of the conversation, while also exasperated by the lack of patience each has for the other's point of view.

Once home, they get to work making a fire, scrubbing the mussels picked that morning, cracking open some more Guinness and wine, and counting out the cowries.

As they sit down to eat, someone will raise a glass, and make a toast to a woman named Jessica, born on that day – 22 July – in 1963, whose strongest loves are sitting around the table, joined by others whom she never knew, but all loved by the ones she loved, in the place she adored more than any other. It will be a toast to how they shared their lives with her, loving her so fiercely and gently as the inexorable march of the invisible cancer cells ate away at her life and took her from them years ago.

Later, they'll drink too much and play games and sing and read books and snooze, and perhaps plan the next day's adventure in whatever the weather brings.

Acknowledgements

They say it takes a village, but I see it a little differently. The way I see it, when life whacks you over – and inside – the head with a brutal disease, there's only one way to get through it: family. Or rather, families. Lots of families.

The first family I'd like to thank for helping me write this memoir is my GBM family. The irony is, you wouldn't wish this illness on your most repulsive, narcissistic, evil, revolting enemy (I won't mention his name). Yet I'm so glad for my own sake that I've shared this journey with some of the most inspiring and courageous people I've ever had the privilege to know. There are so many, including the hundreds of people who are active members of OurBrainBank, and many dear friends who are no longer here for me to thank. Jana Bennett, Adam Hayden, Nancy Kuhn, Meredith Moore, Rod Nordland, Glenn von Nostitz, Jennifer Rosenthal and Theresa Schaub have all been cherished members of my GBM family who have been there with me, and for me, all the way.

I would never have lived long enough to write this book without the exceptional care of my medical family. Over the past five years I have been so lucky to be treated by several of the leading brain specialists in the world. From the first day I met Fabio Iwamoto, neuro-oncologist at Columbia University, he encouraged me to think bigger and be more ambitious about my own response to my brain tumour. I owe him everything for that, and for becoming such a great friend and constant support. Esther Kim, the acute care nurse practitioner at Columbia's Department of Neurology, buoyed me up with her smile and profound care, even when the news was bad.

In Boston, I also received astonishing treatment. David Reardon, Clinical Director of the Center for Neuro-Oncology at Dana-Farber Cancer Institute, is not only a world-leading research scientist at the front lines of new treatments, but he also talks to me as a friend, always in language I can understand and appreciate. Antonio Chiocca, the neurosurgeon in chief of Brigham & Women's Hospital, pumped the herpes virus into my brain, and I loved him for it! The treatment, which is at the frontier of experimental thinking about how to aggressively attack brain tumours using the power of the body's own immune system, didn't work for me – but I have no doubt that it, or future iterations, will do the trick for others who come after me. Jennifer Stefanik and Daniel Triggs, nurse practitioners in Boston, were always there for me.

I'd also like to thank other members of my medical family: Guy McKhann, neurosurgeon at Columbia University; Joshua Silverman of NYU Langone; Mario Lacouture of Memorial Sloan Kettering Cancer Center; and Maurice Beer of Integrative Medical NY. Marina Benaur, a psychiatrist at Columbia University, helped me through my darkest moments. Jennifer Levine of Weill Cornell Medicine was already a good friend before the storm set in, but she gave me hope by refusing to allow me to settle for standard treatment and by insisting I got a second opinion. So I went to see Fabio, and the rest is history . . .

My third family is OurBrainBank. From a standing start, it has grown into an international organisation with huge potential. That has meant so much to me. Having had my working life snatched away, OBB has given me back my sense of purpose. It's one important answer to why I'm still here, five years on. And it would not, could not, have happened without the tireless work and support of so many people. Our board in the US, UK and Australia has been the muscle behind the operation: Jana, Meredith and Theresa, alongside Jake Arnold-Forster, Stacy Chick, Richard Clemmow, Kelli Duprey, Gail Fosler, Julia Hobsbawm, Simon Matthews, Andi Phillips, my husband Ed Pilkington and Claire Wright. They have been driven on by the Herculean efforts of our staff, Aurelia Driver, Stacey Shackford and Martha Wilkie. The brains behind OBB come from our medical and technical advisers: Fabio, David, Antonio, Marina, Joshua and Mario, with Alexis Demopoulos, Bruce Hellman, Lakshmi Nayak and Daniel Orringer.

Then there is my writing family. I never expected to write a book, and this too could never have happened without enormous support. I'm so grateful to my wonderful agent Zoë Pagnamenta, who believed in me and encouraged me in this project all the way. In Ursula Doyle, publisher of Fleet, the literary imprint of Little, Brown, I could not have found a more sensitive and inspiring editor. Sarah Beal of Muswell Press gave me the idea for the memoir in the first place, urging me to take the blogs I was writing to family and friends and build them up into a book. Andy Postman was my writing buddy, cajoling me gently to keep at it, as well as helping me edit the first draft. My nephew Milo Caiger-Smith was my trusted Zoom assistant during the pandemic when I could no longer work on the page myself due to loss of peripheral vision.

We have reached family proper. My amazing nieces and nephews – I love you! My in-laws Karen Taube, Anna and Guy Pilkington and partners – thank you for so much. My brother Ben Morris and sister Frances Morris and their partners, and above all my mother Liz Morris – you have held my hand through it all.

And finally, my family. Ed, we've done this together. All of it. Thirty-seven years and counting. Felix, Tess and Emma. It's all about you in the end. It's always been all about you. You are my flame, and you will carry it for me into the future.

Jessica Morris
January 2021

Afterword

Jessica died at home in Brooklyn at about 10 pm on 8 June 2021. Over the previous several days she had gradually fallen into a coma, her breathing laboured, her chest rising and falling in great convulsive waves.

We had started a night shift after a succession of sleepless nights, three hours on, three hours off, like the crew of one of her beloved boats. We were just preparing for the start of the night, and I was giving Jess the third of her daily intravenous injections.

As I was fussing over her right arm there was a sudden transformation. She took in a large breath, then relaxed. She lost thirty years in that split second. Her face, strained over so many weeks, regained its poise and beauty. She appeared serene; I might even go so far as to say at peace.

I called out and the others joined. Felix, Tess and Emma rushed into our bedroom and held her tight.

Jessica's sister Frances and my sister Anna entered the circle. She took one more breath, as eloquent as any goodbye, and was gone.

It's been months now since that extraordinary, baffling moment and I'm still clueless as to how to answer the obvious question: where did she go? Where did all that energy, all the jokes, all the desires, all the ambition and drive for change, all the love, go? It's as if a dimension has been stripped out from our house, turning its vibrant 3D into a grey, flat sheet.

About a year before Jessica died we had 'the conversation'. I asked her what she wanted to happen after she died. She didn't like the subject one little bit. After all, Jessica was all about beginnings not endings. You could hear the distress in her voice – the reluctance to go there – but with characteristic courage she stuck with it and set out for me a basic plan for how to mark her life.

And so it was that the children and I found ourselves in July making our way to Heir Island in Ireland, her spiritual home, carrying a box with half her ashes. I've been going to this tiny island in an archipelago off the coast of Cork since 1984, the year our relationship began, and I can count on my fingers the number of blazing summers we enjoyed in that time. Far more common, as Jessica writes on an earlier page, was weather of the sort known as 'soft' – fine drizzle under darkened skies.

It was Sod's law that the one year Jessica couldn't be

there, Heir Island exploded into Mediterranean glory. The sea was turquoise, the beaches glistened in the sunshine. She had wanted her ashes scattered at the cowrie beach, the setting of her epilogue, but in the end we opted for a beautiful enclosed inlet looking west to the Fastnet Rock and, fittingly, to America beyond. We named it 'Jessica's Beach'. Seventeen members of the extended Morris family gathered there under a sweltering sun. Felix, Tess, Emma and I waded waist-high into the balmy water and let our Jess's ashes float out and melt into the sea, creating a wispy cloud that wrapped its arms around us.

The other half of the ashes we buried the day before Thanksgiving under a young red maple in Prospect Park.

Jessica also laid down plans for celebrations in New York and London which we held in October and November respectively. At each, family and friends shared stories, there was singing from her old choirs, and the kids read extracts of *All In My Head*: Emma on Greenwich, Felix on Nicaragua and Tess on patient power. At the New York celebration, Fabio Iwamoto gave a key address which in itself was an expression of the extraordinary bridge Jessica built between patient and doctor.

Fabio pointed out that even after death Jessica kept up the fight: she donated her brain to medical research. Scientists studied her tissue in both Columbia and Harvard – a collaboration between experts that was another of Jessica's hallmarks.

'Jessica finally found her voice in fighting for better treatments and for patients to be heard,' Fabio said. 'That voice was loud and beautiful. Jessica, we heard you, we will continue your work.'

So what have we left after the ashes were scattered, the celebrations held, the speeches delivered? We have a house that is unnaturally empty, echoing with silence where once there was laughter and song. We have Jessica's clothes gathering dust in the closet, shelves of adored novels that will never be read again, a dog missing her best friend.

Yet even I – the glass half empty to Jessica's half full – must acknowledge that she left us so much more than that. We have the children, who are tearing into life with undiminished effervescence despite the bitter blow of losing their mother – a genetic trait that without doubt stems from her.

We have Jessica's Beach, and the maple tree where we and her legion of friends will picnic on summer days.

We have OurBrainBank which despite – because of – her absence is steaming ahead, striving to turn GBM from terminal to treatable powered by patients. We will defeat you, TEF!

We have the hundreds of letters of condolence that poured through the letter box, bursting with stories from all periods of Jessica's life. They included personal letters to the children and me from two world leaders, on either side of the pond.

Gordon Brown, the former British prime minister who knew Jessica through their mutual friend Sheila McKechnie, wrote a touching letter by hand, saying 'Jessica achieved so much despite her illness, and she has done a huge amount to help fellow sufferers'.

Joe Biden sent not one but two letters from the White House – one to me and another separate note to Tess, Felix and Emma. The US President raised the shared experience of losing someone to GBM, in his case his son Beau who died a year before Jessica was diagnosed.

'Jessica spent her life helping others, refusing to relent even when she became ill,' he wrote to the kids. 'She was an incredible mother, protective and loving of you three. Her efforts were extraordinary and so important to patients and families, including ours, who have faced GBM.'

Biden has been afflicted with more bereavement in his life than is imaginable. So when he talked to the children about coping with grief, his words resonated.

'Though the grieving process never quite ends, I promise that the day will come when your mother's memory will bring a smile to your lips before it brings a tear to your eye. My prayer for you is that this day comes sooner rather than later.'

Jessica would firmly approve that sentiment. Indeed, that's another thing that she has bequeathed us. We have her voice ringing in our ears, gently reprimanding us for moping over her loss. There is too much to be done, too many injustices to be fought, friends to be supported, chats to be had, illnesses to be tackled, to mope around.

And there's one more thing that she left us. Now we have this book. To hold in our hands, to revel in the physicality of its pages. Open it up and her words soar out, urging us on in that irrepressible Jessica way: Everything is possible. Nothing is insurmountable. Love it all. Go for it!

Ed Pilkington
Brooklyn
February 2022

APPENDIX

OurBrainBank

Website: ourbrainbank.org

Jessica Morris founded OurBrainBank in the US in 2018 as a non-profit dedicated to moving glioblastoma from terminal to treatable, powered by patients. From a standing start it has grown into an international organisation with branches in the US, the UK and Australia. It now has a global membership of thousands of people with GBM, their carers, families and friends – an extraordinary achievement for such a rare disease. OurBrainBank helps patients better manage their illness and together have a collective voice and strength that Jessica always hoped would change the course of this terrible cancer.

OurBrainBank has a medical advisory panel including some of the world's leading neuro-oncologists and surgeons. It is a mark of Jessica's powers of persuasion that her own physicians and surgeon – Fabio Iwamoto of Columbia University and David Reardon and Antonio Chiocca of Harvard Medical School – are all central members of the advisory group.

Having established an active user group of hundreds of patients, OurBrainBank has expanded to create a Bill of Rights for people living with GBM. The organisation aims to support patients as they negotiate the extreme challenges of living with GBM. It also mobilises their untapped patient power to put pressure on the medical profession, big pharma and government to speed up the search for a desperately needed cure.

To support the work and growth of OurBrainBank, you can donate at ourbrainbank.org/give/

Credits

Chapter 4

'Your Attention Please' from *Collected Poems* by Peter Porter. Copyright © The Estate of Peter Porter. Reproduced by permission of the Estate c/o Rogers, Coleridge & White Ltd., 20 Powis Mews, London W11 1JN.

Louis MacNeice, 'Snow' from *The Collected Poems of Louis MacNeice*. Copyright © The Estate of Louis MacNeice. Reprinted by permission of David Higham Associates Ltd.

Chapter 6

Derek Mahon, 'Everything Is Going to Be Alright' from *Selected Poems*. Copyright © 1991 by Derek Mahon. Reprinted with the permission of The Gallery Press.